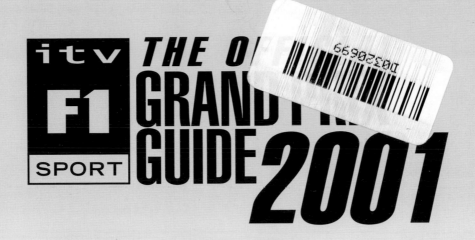

itv F1 SPORT

THE OFFICIAL GRAND PRIX GUIDE 2001

THIS IS A CARLTON BOOK

This edition published in 2001

10 9 8 7 6 5 4 3 2 1

Text and design copyright © Carlton Books Limited 2001

A CIP catalogue record for this book is available from the British Library

The publisher has taken reasonable steps to check the accuracy
of the facts contained herein at the time of going to press but
can take no responsibility for any errors

ISBN paperback 1 84222 197 3
ISBN hardback 1 84222 364 X

Project Editor: Kerrin Edwards
Project Art Direction: Mark Lloyd
Designed by: Phil Gambrill
Production: Lisa French
Picture Research: Debora Fioravanti

Printed in Italy

Carlton Books Ltd. would like to thank the following sources for their
kind permission to reproduce the pictures in this book:

Allsport UK Ltd 32, 55, 57/ Graham Chadwick 85, Robert Cianflone 52,
Michael Cooper 65, 76, Robert Laberge 4r, Clive Mason 3, 5l, 6-7, 12, 15, 16, 17,
25, 41, 42, 44, 64, 86, 90, 91, 96, 97,100tl, 100bl, 117, Pascal Rondeau 122,
124, Tom Shaw 93, Mark Thompson 2, 4r, 5r, 19, 24, 28, 30, 33, 37, 43, 45, 51,
62-3, 66, 67, 69, 71, 72, 73, 74, 75, 77, 80, 81, 84, 89, 92, 95, 100c, 104, 108,
114 ,119
Empics/John Marsh 8-9, 34, 47, 48, 50, 100tr, 101, 103, 106, 109, 110, 112,
113, 115, 118, Antti Puskala 100-1, 111
ITV Network 6
LAT Photographic 10, 11, 13, 14, 18, 20, 21, 22, 23, 26, 27, 29, 31, 35, 36, 38,
39, 40, 46, 49, 53, 54, 56l, 56r, 68, 70, 78, 79, 82, 83, 87, 88, 94, 98-9, 102,
105, 107,116,123, 125
PA News Photo Library/ Michael Stephens 128

Every effort has been made to acknowledge correctly and contact the source
and/or copyright holder of each picture, and Carlton Books Limited apologizes
for any unintentional errors or omissions which will be corrected in future
editions of this book.

THE OFFICIAL
GRAND PRIX
GUIDE 2001

itv F1 SPORT

Bruce Jones

CARLTON
BOOKS

F1 CONTENTS

Chapter 2

Chapter 3

Chapter 4

Chapter 5

MURRAY WALKER

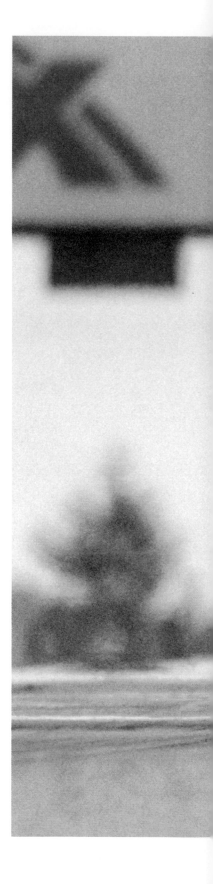

I am an eternal optimist and every year I convince myself that the next season is going to be even better than the last. Whatever happens in 2001 it is going to be very special for me because, after 52 years of TV commentary, I have decided it is to be my last. I don't want to stop but I'm determined to do so whilst I'm still ahead with the viewers rather than wait until they think I'm past it and I have a gut feeling that now is the time to wind down. However, I have no doubt that I'm going to have a wonderful final year, because although 2000 was a season to savour, with Michael Schumacher at last winning Ferrari's first Driver's Championship since 1979 and the Prancing Horse team doing the double with their second successive Constructors' title, it looks like 2001 will witness even fiercer competition. For, as ever, there are changes to the teams, their cars and their drivers, which could result in Ferrari and McLaren – who have both dominated Grand Prix racing since 1997 – being given more of a run for their money this time around.

I'll be surprised if Schumacher, Barrichello, Hakkinen and Coulthard who, between them, won every race last year, fail to scoop up most of the victories, but I'll be equally surprised if they win them all. Because I am expecting Williams in particular to be a major threat. Despite two new elements last year, BMW engines and Jenson Button, Williams had an incredibly successful season. No-one expected them to take third place in the Constructors' Championship with a new engine from a manufacturer that had been out of Formula One since 1983. But they did, and with another new, second generation motor from BMW, they could be challenging for wins. Yet, whether their decision to replace the amazing Button with Colombian ChampCar ace Juan Pablo Montoya proves to be a wise move remains to be seen. For what it's worth I think he will be sensational.

There are three other teams I expect to be closer to the front in 2001: Jordan, BAR and Benetton. Jordan had a dismal 2000 for them, due to poor reliability, but with official Honda works engines and the driving talents of Heinz-Harald Frentzen and Jarno Trulli, they could be winners. The same applies to BAR as 1997 Champion Jacques Villeneuve will be partnered by past Grand Prix victor Olivier Panis – hungry for success after his rejuvenating stint as McLaren's test driver. To complete my Top Teams there's Benetton, who have a much-vaunted innovatory engine from their new owners Renault and are determined to return to Formula One where they left it – at the top. With Jenson Button partnering Giancarlo Fisichella they could indeed do so, and I'm confident that, with the experience of his brilliant debut season behind him, Jenson will be even more competitive than he was last year.

Such is the fierceness of the competition in Formula One that I feel the other teams – Jaguar, Prost, Arrows, Sauber and Minardi – will do well to score points, but there's a major change in 2001 that could make a mockery of my expectations: the return of Michelin. The French tyre maker has dominated Formula One in the past and, given that the right tyres can beneficially affect lap times even more than extra power, the Michelin-shod teams could do better against their Bridgestone-equipped rivals than expected. And two of those Michelin teams are Williams and Benetton.

So, all in all it looks like interesting times ahead and that I'll be going out on a high!

Those who thought that McLaren would come out on top in 2000 after setting the pace throughout close season testing were proved wrong. Will this year see them fight back to regain the supremacy from Ferrari? Or will another team shift up a gear or two to challenge for outright honours? This is one of the many questions that Formula One fans the world over will be asking as the weeks are ticked off to the first of the forthcoming World Championship's 17 sets of starting lights are extinguished in Melbourne in March. No two seasons are ever the same, so look forward with us to the new mix of factors assembled for your delectation for the season ahead.

With status quo being maintained on the driver front at both Ferrari and McLaren, with Michael Schumacher and Rubens Barrichello again facing Mika Hakkinen and David Coulthard for Ferrari and McLaren respectively, it's a case of the same again in 2001, so it's up to the designers and engine suppliers to do their best to change the order. Indeed, a tyre war is brewing between Bridgestone and incoming Michelin – back for the first time since the mid-1980s – but neither Ferrari nor McLaren have switched to the new

FERRARI MCLAREN WILLIAMS BENETTON B.A.R.

French rubber, so that's another variable removed from the equation, making it all the more likely that Formula One fans will be able to enjoy some more epic battles between these four drivers.

Traction control is set to be reintroduced from the Spanish GP onwards in 2001, if the teams can prove it can be policed properly. So this might jumble up the order slightly, but whether any other teams or drivers can get close to Ferrari and McLaren remains to be seen. Of the opposition, Williams must fancy its chances in its second season with BMW engines. The German manufacturer was conservative in its engine specification in 2000, so expect a leap in horsepower this time around, with Ralf Schumacher sure to be on his toes to keep the incoming Juan Pablo Montoya behind him, especially as he found his authority questioned by rookie Jenson Button's pace last year.

Benetton will most likely start to impress with Renault's revolutionary new engine, offering Button the chance to put one over the team that let him go: Williams. While Giancarlo Fisichella will be giving his all to score that first win that has eluded him for so long, as his chances of staying on with a top team into 2002 will dwindle further if he is outpaced by his new team-mate, since team boss Flavio Briatore suggested last year that Fisichella doesn't always deliver the goods.

Works Honda engines helped BAR to equal fourth overall in last year's Constructors' Cup, but this year they will not be alone in using the Japanese engines as Jordan's Jarno Trulli and Heinz-Harald Frentzen will also have them in the rear of their cars, presumably offering more grunt than the Mugen Honda engines they used last year. However, BAR's Jacques Villeneuve and Olivier Panis - reinvigorated by a year of stunning testing performances with McLaren - will be out to win this battle within a battle. Behind this group will probably come Jaguar, desperate to improve on its unimpressive debut last year, with Eddie Irvine hoping that last year's car's basic imbalance has been sorted. Team-mate Luciano Burti will simply be anxious to get in some Grand Prix mileage.

Arrows showed greater promise than Jaguar last year, although many a strong drive ended with retirement, but its move to AMT-badged Peugeot engines may help Pedro de la Rosa and Jos Verstappen in their quest to fight their way clear of the midfield. However, a lack of budget could well hamper the team's progress. This then brings us to the likely stragglers at the tail of field: Sauber, Prost and Minardi. Sauber's hopes rest with Nick Heidfeld and Finnish hotshot Kimi Raikkonen, who has leapt direct from Formula Renault, while Prost will be hoping that its ex-Ferrari engines can inspire Jean Alesi and team-mate to great things. The close season proved to be a long one for Minardi as the little Italian team endured a host of disappointments, such as losing their sponsor. To expect much of the two Minardi drivers is to expect too much. Survival may be all that they can hope for.

However, 17 Grands Prix at 17 circuits around the globe are sure to provide another epic battle for outright honours and no few surprises along the way.

FERRARI

SAME AGAIN PLEASE

Ferrari "got the monkey off its back" last year by leading Michael Schumacher to the coveted drivers' title. This year the world's most popular team will be looking to do the same again, and has every chance of doing so.

THE MAIN MAN: Ross Brawn is more than simply Ferrari's technical director, as he calls their race tactics from the pit wall

Jean Todt was able to walk tall at the end of last year, having survived countless palace coups to complete seven years of work to turn Ferrari around into a team capable not only of winning Grands Prix with regularity, but also to give Ferrari its first drivers' champion since Jody Scheckter in 1979.

If the team can have the same start as last year – three wins from the first three races – then there's no reason why they can't come out on top again. Michael Schumacher will certainly be up for it, and Rubens Barrichello too. Indeed, while the Brazilian was delighted to score his first win last year, he was less than happy to be the number two, and will be going all out to prove that he's worthy of equal equipment, making the team environment a healthily competitive one – unless Barrichello feels that he's being marginalized, as Schumacher's team-mates sometimes have been in the past.

SHOOTS LIKE AN ARROW

Last year's Ferrari F1-2000 was the best Ferrari chassis ever, with the greatest advance coming from its aerodynamics.

The gains that designer Rory Byrne made in this area enabled the car to be more responsive to change, and thus more easily tailored to each circuit. With its traditional helping of Ferrari horsepower – to say nothing of Schumacher's driving talents – the F1-2000 was to be found on pole position more times than the McLaren, winning ten to seven, and thus reversing the recent trend.

Schumacher couldn't have asked for more from the first three rounds, picking up three wins. On top of that, McLaren exhibited an unusual level of frailty. New team-mate Barrichello showed himself to be a capable number two who was rather closer to Schumacher's pace than Eddie Irvine had been. Well, at least some of the time. Like Irvine, though, he was a consistent scorer, starting with second place in Melbourne and losing out on his maiden victory at Silverstone with hydraulic failure.

A HAPPY MAN: Ferrari president Luca di Montezemolo felt a dream had been achieved last year

Schumacher was at his best to win at a damp Nurburgring, and was heading for his fifth victory of the season at Monaco when his rear suspension failed. A Ferrari won in Montreal, but team orders dictated that it was Schumacher's, with Barrichello told to hold station behind as his team leader suffered with a brake problem. But then Schumacher's season took a dive. Passed by Coulthard at Magny-Cours, his engine blew. Then, trying to be let past Barrichello into the first corner in Austria, he was hit from behind by Ricardo Zonta and was out on the spot. Two weeks later, he also failed to negotiate the first corner at Hockenheim, letting his challengers from McLaren close in. At least Ferrari came away from Hockenheim with a win, though, as Barrichello was helped when a spectator broke onto the track, bringing out the safety car, and then drove an inspired race as track conditions changed. A pair of second places for Schumacher behind Hakkinen at the Hungaroring and Spa-Francorchamps were followed by three straight wins, at Monza, Indianapolis and Suzuka – the third of these giving him the drivers' title that a Ferrari driver (Jody Scheckter) had last won in 1979. Schumacher then fought from behind Coulthard to round off the season at Sepang with a fourth straight win. And this was enough to give Ferrari the Constructors' Cup for the second successive year.

IN AT THE START

Ferrari has by far the longest history of any Formula One team, having been involved from the first World Championship in 1950. Thus it's not surprising that the team has amassed more wins than any other – albeit by only a handful from McLaren, a team that made its debut in 1966. Run down a list of Ferrari's 10 World Champions – Alberto Ascari (1952 and 1953), Juan Manuel Fangio (1956), Mike Hawthorn (1958), Phil Hill (1961), John Surtees (1964), Niki Lauda (1975 and 1977), Jody Scheckter (1979) and Schumacher – and add those to its 10 Constructors' Cups, and the team's pedigree is plain. Ferrari has also fielded other greats who didn't come away with the crown, including Peter Collins, Wolfgang von Trips, Chris Amon, Jacky Ickx, Clay Regazzoni, Gilles Villeneuve, Michele Alboreto, Nigel Mansell, Gerhard Berger and Jean Alesi. However, for all its funding from parent company, Fiat, success hasn't always been guaranteed, with its top-heavy management structure having to be cleared out in the late 1990s to help the team find its way again under president Luca di Montezemolo.

FOR THE RECORD

Country of origin	Italy
Team base	Maranello, Italy
Date of formation	1939
Active years in Formula One	From 1950
Grands Prix contested	636
Wins	135
Pole positions	137
Fastest laps	144
Constructors' Cup victories	1961, 1964, 1975, 1976, 1977, 1979, 1982, 1983, 1999, 2000

DRIVERS + RESULTS 2000

Driver	Nationality	Races	Wins	Pts	Pos
Michael Schumacher	German	17	9	108	1st
Rubens Barrichello	Brazilian	17	1	62	4th

CAR SPECIFICATIONS

Sponsors	Marlboro, Shell, TIM, Tic Tac
Team principal	Jean Todt
Technical director	Ross Brawn
Team manager	Stefano Domenicali
Designer	Rory Byrne
Chief engineer	Giorgio Ascanelli
Test driver	Luca Badoer
Chassis	Ferrari F1-2001
Engine	Ferrari V10
Tyres	Bridgestone

GOING AFTER RECORDS

Michael Schumacher brought five years of work to fruition last year when he finally became World Champion for Ferrari. He now ranks second in the all-time winners list, and the number-one position is his target for 2001.

TRACK NOTES

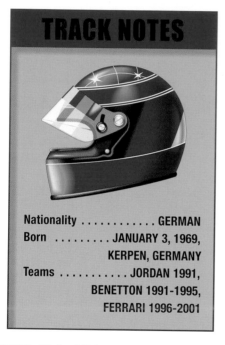

Nationality . . . . GERMAN
Born . . . . JANUARY 3, 1969,
KERPEN, GERMANY
Teams . . . . JORDAN 1991,
BENETTON 1991-1995,
FERRARI 1996-2001

LOOKING TO THE STARS: Michael Schumacher joined the ranks of three-time Champions in 2000

A lain Prost holds the record number of Grand Prix wins with 51. Michael Schumacher now has 44, having overhauled the late Ayrton Senna when he won last year's United States Grand Prix.

Michael's exertions last year have added a further £10 million to his annual pay packet, taking it out to beyond £40 million. It's a fortune, but Michael was at his best in 2000, with his performance startling when tracks became wet. To the disappointment of many, his brilliance was matched by his robust driving tactics at Imola, Barcelona, Magny-Cours, Spa-Francorchamps and Suzuka.

Michael made a dream start to last year with three wins in a row. These were even more valuable as the McLarens struggled. Much of this advantage was negated by three straight retirements at Magny-Cours, the A1-Ring and Hockenheim. He was depressed after being outrun by Hakkinen at Spa, but bounced back to win Ferrari's home race at Monza. Victory at Indianapolis put him eight points ahead with two races to go, but Michael turned a likely second place into victory at Suzuka when he and Ross Brawn combined to make the most of a sudden shower to move him ahead of Hakkinen. Victory gave him the crown with a round to run.

METEORIC PROGRESS

Michael leapt from karts to cars in 1988. Propelled into Formula Three in 1989 by manager Willi Weber, Michael ended up third overall, one point behind the champion. He made amends by dominating the German series the following year, also beating Hakkinen to win the Macau street race. He was a works Mercedes sportscar racer in 1991, but made his Formula One debut with Jordan. Snapped up by Benetton for the following race, he stayed with the team until quitting for Ferrari at the end of 1995, by which time he had won two world titles. Progress was slow as Ferrari rebuilt itself in 1996, but he still won some Grands Prix. In the following two seasons, he was in with a shot at the title in the final round, but lost out to Jacques Villeneuve and then Hakkinen. A broken leg at Silverstone took Michael out for six races in 1999, but then came the Championship in 2000...

CAREER RECORD

First Grand Prix . .	1991 BELGIAN GP
Grand Prix starts	 145
Grand Prix wins	 44

1992 Belgian GP, 1993 Portuguese GP,
1994 Brazilian GP, 1994 Pacific GP,
1994 San Marino GP, 1994 Monaco GP,
1994 Canadian GP, 1994 French GP,
1994 Hungarian GP, 1994 European GP,
1995 Brazilian GP, 1995 Spanish GP,
1995 Monaco GP, 1995 French GP,
1995 German GP, 1995 Belgian GP,
1995 European GP, 1995 Pacific GP,
1995 Japanese GP, 1996 Spanish GP,
1996 Belgian GP, 1996 Italian GP, 1997
Monaco GP, 1997 Canadian GP,
1997 French GP, 1997 Belgian GP,
1997 Japanese GP, 1998 Argentinian GP,
1998 Canadian GP, 1998 French GP,
1998 British GP, 1998 Hungarian GP,
1998 Italian GP, 1999 San Marino GP,
1999 Monaco GP, 2000 Australian GP,
2000 Brazilian GP, 2000 San Marino GP,
2000 European GP, 2000 Canadian GP,
2000 Italian GP, 2000 US GP,
2000 Japanese GP, 2000 Malaysian GP

Poles 32
Fastest laps 40
Points 678
Honours . . . . 2000, 1995 & 1994

WORLD CHAMPION, 1990 GERMAN
FORMULA THREE CHAMPION &
MACAU GP WINNER, 1988 GERMAN
FORMULA KONIG CHAMPION

RUBENS BARRICHELLO

MORE WINS WANTED

Rubens Barrichello scored his first Grand Prix win for Ferrari last year and now he wants to win more – to emerge from the shadow of Ferrari team leader Michael Schumacher, and even have a crack at the title himself.

A WINNER: Rubens Barrichello had every right to be emotional when he finally scored his first win last year on his 124th Grand Prix outing

TRACK NOTES

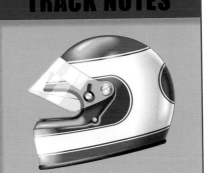

Nationality .... BRAZILIAN
Born .... MAY 23, 1972,
SAO PAULO, BRAZIL
Teams ...... JORDAN 1993-1996,
STEWART 1997-1999,
FERRARI 2000-2001

CAREER RECORD

First Grand Prix ..... 1993 SOUTH
AFRICAN GP
Grand Prix starts 130
Grand Prix wins 1
2000 German GP
Poles 3
Fastest laps 3
Points 139
Honours .. 1991 BRITISH FORMULA
THREE CHAMPION, 1990 EUROPEAN
FORMULA OPEL CHAMPION, 1988
BRAZILIAN KARTING CHAMPION

Rubens Barrichello ended last year in a career-best fourth place overall in the World Championship but, although he tried to hide it, maybe he wasn't completely happy. Sure, he'd won a Grand Prix for the first time, but he was occasionally disillusioned with the support role he was having to play at Ferrari. He didn't expect to be number one ahead of Michael Schumacher, but he wanted equal equipment. How Rubens has wintered with this dissatisfaction will be important to his mental preparedness for 2001. Hopefully, Ferrari will have convinced him that he will take over as number one when Michael retires. But that could be several years away.

On the positive side, Rubens was closer to Michael's pace than Irvine had been over the previous four years, outqualifying him twice, but there were races when he was nowhere near. And there were others when he seemed to be being used as a guinea-pig for race tactics. He also had to hang back in second place at Montreal in support of his team leader. However, all that was forgotten when he scored that first win at the German Grand Prix, a race that had qualifying jumbled by rain. Rubens advanced from 18th and was helped when a spectator broke onto trackside, bringing out the safety car. The emotion of finally winning after 124 starts was all too much for the Brazilian.

BACKED TO SUCCEED

Rubens was such a hotshot in Brazilian karting that a group of businessmen financed his passage to Formula One with the expectation of future returns. He dominated the Formula Opel Euroseries in 1990, then pipped David Coulthard to the 1991 British Formula Three title. After a year of Formula 3000 in which he ranked third overall, Rubens made it to Formula One with Jordan shortly before his 21st birthday. That he ran second to Ayrton Senna in the European Grand Prix on his third outing was remarkable. His car failed with a few laps to go, and this was the start of three years of dashed hopes, with only the odd result such as second in the 1995 Canadian Grand Prix to sustain him.

Stewart Grand Prix was established for 1996, with Rubens as its number-one driver, and he raced to second at Monaco, but all too often retired when the equipment failed him. The 1998 season was even less fruitful. Then, in 1999, Rubens was on the podium three times, but had to smile when it was Johnny Herbert rather than him who gave Stewart its first win.

McLAREN

LOOKING FOR PERFECTION

McLaren has spent the winter working out how it lost out to Ferrari last year and the ultra-professional team from Woking is bound to come back stronger this year, with an eye on not making the tactical mistakes that toppled them in 2000. Their rivals should be quaking.

By McLaren's standards, the team's 2000 campaign was less than satisfactory. They won seven times, but that accounted for fewer than half the races, and it allowed Ferrari's Michael Schumacher to win nine times and prevent Mika Hakkinen from being the first driver since Juan Manuel Fangio to win the drivers' title three years running. Tactical blunders and mechanical failures cost them dear,

and helped Schumacher escape. Indeed, no sooner had Schumacher beaten Hakkinen to the drivers' title than Mercedes blamed itself for the engine failures that cost Hakkinen victory when leading the first two races – giving Schumacher a flying start – and again when the Finn's engine failed at Indianapolis. So, you can be sure that Ilmor, the company that builds the Mercedes engines, won't let that happen again.

THE VIPS

RON DENNIS

A mechanic for Cooper in the mid-1960s, Ron worked for Brabham before forming the Rondel Formula Two team in 1971. He landed a contract in 1979 to run 25 BMW M1s in a one-make series, and his Project Four concern combined with Marlboro to take over McLaren in 1980. He took sole control in 1982, and his drivers have since claimed nine drivers' titles.

ADRIAN NEWEY

This aerodynamicist's first job in Formula One was with Fittipaldi in 1980. After joining March, he worked in Formula Two, sportscars and then ChampCar racing with Truesports. His return to Formula One was with March before he joined Williams in 1990, helping the team to its strongest period, before moving on to McLaren in 1997.

THE BRAINS OF F1: Adrian Newey is the designer that every teams wants on its books

One thing that can be taken for granted is that designer Adrian Newey will have produced the most aerodynamically efficient chassis for 2001. His track record speaks for itself, as shown by the world titles his drivers at Williams then McLaren have achieved. His ability to produce a design that works in the wind tunnel considerably sooner than other aerodynamicists manage is one of his strong suits.

Continuity and experience have long been key to McLaren's success. To this end, both Hakkinen and David Coulthard are staying on for a record sixth season together, making theirs the longest partnership in history. In fact, Hakkinen has been a McLaren man since 1993.

TOO MANY FAILURES

The first sign of trouble came when both cars retired from the opening round. Hakkinen retired again at Interlagos, a race in which Coulthard was disqualified from second for a front-wing irregularity. A good result was needed at Imola to

Champion. James Hunt then followed suit in 1976, but McLaren slipped into decline before current boss Ron Dennis took control in 1980.

John Barnard's ground-breaking designs and the arrival of Niki Lauda and Alain Prost made the team invincible in 1984 and 1985, with Prost using his legendary guile to nick the title from the Williams drivers in 1986. Ayrton Senna and Prost shared the titles between 1988 and 1991, three-one in favour of Senna, before McLaren slipped from the sport's pinnacle. Its catalyst to return to the top came with a partnership with Mercedes, with wins starting in the opening race of 1997 before Hakkinen claimed the 1998 and 1999 titles.

BROTHERS IN ARMS: McLaren boss Ron Dennis has had a special relationship with Hakkinen since his Adelaide crash

atone for this, but the McLarens were beaten in a straight fight by Schumacher.

A pair of one-twos at Silverstone and Barcelona put McLaren back on track, with Coulthard fortunate to be racing at all after surviving a plane crash that killed his pilot and co-pilot. But Schumacher's ability on a slippery track helped him beat both McLaren drivers at the Nurburgring. McLaren came up trumps at Monaco, though, when Coulthard finally got past Jarno Trulli's Jordan, and his pursuit of Schumacher was rewarded when Ferrari failed and he swept through to win.

A stop-go penalty in Montreal cost Coulthard a possible win, but he put on a storming drive to victory at Magny-Cours, overpowering Schumacher. Having been less focused than usual, Hakkinen was allowed a brief break and came back to lead home a McLaren one-two at the A1-Ring. They were looking good for another at Hockenheim until a spectator broke onto the circuit and brought out the safety car, with Barrichello then reading mixed conditions best and passing Hakkinen to win. McLaren bungled its tactics for Coulthard, and did so again when rain hit the Belgian Grand Prix. Luckily, consecutive wins for Hakkinen in Hungary and Belgium put him six points clear of Schumacher, but the German outraced him at Monza. At Indianapolis, Hakkinen was second and closing when his engine failed, leaving him eight points adrift going to Suzuka. He had to win, but Schumacher overhauled him with a better pit-stop strategy. McLaren's hopes of taking maximum points at Sepang and relying on Ferrari not scoring more than two points were scotched when Hakkinen moved before the starting lights went out and his stop-go penalty handed matters to Ferrari, even though Coulthard pushed Schumacher all the way to the finish.

A HISTORY OF SUCCESS

If he were alive today, Bruce McLaren would be extremely proud of what his team has achieved. Before the Kiwi racer/engineer died in a testing accident in 1970, McLaren had won numerous CanAm sportscar titles, but only four Grands Prix since its debut in 1966. Since then, it has added another 130 wins to challenge Ferrari at the top of the table. With Teddy Mayer at the helm, McLaren won three Grands Prix in 1973, but moved up a gear in 1974 when Emerson Fittipaldi arrived and promptly became McLaren's first World

FOR THE RECORD

Country of origin	England
Team base	Woking, England
Date of formation	1963
Active years in Formula One	From 1966
Grands Prix contested	509
Wins	130
Pole positions	110
Fastest laps	101
Constructors' Cup victories	1974, 1984, 1985, 1988, 1989, 1990, 1991, 1998

DRIVERS + RESULTS 2000

Driver	Nationality	Races	Wins	Pts	Pos
Mika Hakkinen	Finnish	17	4	89	2nd
David Coulthard	Scottish	17	3	73	3rd

CAR SPECIFICATIONS

Sponsors	West, Mercedes, Mobil, Computer Associates, Loctite
Team principal	Ron Dennis
Team manager	David Ryan
Designer	Adrian Newey
Chief engineer	Steve Hallam
Test driver	Alexander Wurz
Chassis	McLaren MP4-16
Engine	Mercedes V10
Tyres	Bridgestone

MIKA HAKKINEN

BEATEN BUT NOT BOWED

Mika Hakkinen didn't enjoy being prevented from making it three world titles in a row last year, so rest assured that he and McLaren will be giving it their all in the campaign ahead, focused on putting Ferrari back behind them.

COOL OPERATOR: Mika Hakkinen stayed level-headed in defeat last year but wants to be Champion again in 2001

Last year was a peculiar year for Mika. He scored no points in the first two races, despite leading both of them. He was then beaten by Michael Schumacher at Imola and found himself 24 points adrift. Victory at Barcelona seemed to have put him back on track, but it was followed by a strange period in which Mika was no longer outrunning team-mate David Coulthard as he had done before. Mika then took a break, and people said the rest did him good as he bounced back to win at the A1-Ring and the Hungaroring. He would have won at Hockenheim, too, had it not been for a track invader bringing out the safety car and wiping out his lead.

Then Mika pulled off the "Move of the Century" at the Belgian Grand Prix when he took the lead. He'd been chopped by Michael Schumacher on the previous lap, but executed a fabulous move when Schumacher passed Ricardo Zonta's BAR into Les Combes and Mika nipped through a tiny gap on the other side, emerging ahead of the Ferrari.

He then had to settle for second place behind Schumacher at Monza, and he was closing in on the German at Indianapolis when his engine blew. This meant he had to win at Suzuka in order to keep his title hopes alive, but Schumacher's inspired form in a rain shower dropped him to second in a pit-stop sequence, and that was that. Admirably, Mika was gracious in defeat. Any chance of revenge at Sepang was blown when he jumped the start – a stop-go penalty confining him to 18th – and he did well to recover to fourth.

A CHAMPION ALL THE WAY

There was very little that Mika didn't win in the junior formulae. Formula Ford and Formula Opel offered up titles in successive years before he took two goes to become British Formula Three Champion in 1990. Impressed by his obvious speed, Lotus signed him up for the 1991 World Championship. He showed well, but Lotus was on the decline and Mika leapt at a chance to join McLaren in 1993. However, Ayrton Senna changed his mind about leaving and Mika was kept on the sidelines until Michael Andretti was dropped. Mika promptly outqualified Senna... Mika endured a life-threatening head injury at Adelaide in 1995 and was ready when McLaren rediscovered its winning form in 1997. Fifth that year, Mika followed it up by winning the world title in 1998 and 1999.

TRACK NOTES

Nationality . . . . FINNISH
Born . . . . . . SEPTEMBER 28, 1968,
HELSINKI, FINLAND
Teams . . . . LOTUS 1991-1992,
McLAREN 1993-2001

CAREER RECORD

First Grand Prix . . . . . . 1991 US GP
Grand Prix starts 145
Grand Prix wins 18
1997 European GP,
1998 Australian GP,
1998 Brazilian GP,
1998 Spanish GP, 1998 Monaco GP,
1998 Austrian GP, 1998 German GP,
1998 Luxembourg GP,
1998 Japanese GP,
1999 Brazilian GP,
1999 Spanish GP, 1999 Canadian GP,
1999 Hungarian GP,
1999 Japanese GP,
2000 Spanish GP, 2000 Austrian GP,
2000 Hungarian GP,
2000 Belgian GP
Poles 26
Fastest laps 22
Points 383
Honours: . . . . 1999 & 1998
WORLD CHAMPION,
1990 BRITISH FORMULA
THREE CHAMPION,
1988 EUROPEAN FORMULA
OPEL CHAMPION,
1987 SCANDINAVIAN FORMULA
FORD CHAMPION,
1986 FINNISH KARTING CHAMPION

DAVID COULTHARD

THWARTED AMBITION

David Coulthard had his best shot yet at becoming World Champion last year. But it didn't work out, and now he must start all over again. This won't be easy either, as his McLaren team-mate Mika Hakkinen has regained the upper hand.

D avid Coulthard told everyone there would be "no more Mr Nice Guy" in 2000. He was putting the focus solely on his quest to put one over team-mate Mika Hakkinen and go for the title.

The trouble was, if there was bad luck to be had at McLaren, it was David who suffered it. He was disqualified from second at Interlagos as his front wing was knocked askew and hung too low. He dropped to seventh in Montreal after a stop-go penalty for his car being worked on after the 15-second board on the grid. In between, he won at Silverstone.

What happened next seemed to stiffen his resolve. David was involved in a plane crash before the Spanish Grand Prix in which his pilot and co-pilot died. Driving with broken ribs, he made a valiant comeback to finish second at Barcelona.

David was on pole at the Nurburgring and won at Monaco after Michael Schumacher retired. He then put in a storming drive to victory at Magny-Cours, overpowering Schumacher's Ferrari. But he suffered at Hockenheim – where he qualified on pole by 1.4 seconds in the rain – when a spectator broke onto the circuit, and he had to stay out for a lap while team-mate Hakkinen pitted for rain tyres. The time he lost as a result consigned him to third. He suffered a similar misfortune at Spa-Francorchamps as McLaren again favoured Hakkinen.

To keep his title hopes alive David had to win at Monza, but he was taken out on the first lap, and his role thereafter would be to support Hakkinen. A jump-start earned him a stop-go penalty at Indianapolis, and he could only fight back to fifth from 15th. Then he was left in the wake of the title challengers in a distant third at Suzuka before fighting back by chasing Schumacher to the flag at Sepang.

SUCCESS ALL THE WAY

David arrived in Formula Ford in 1989 as a karting champion and proceeded to show why. He finished runner-up to Rubens Barrichello in British Formula Three in 1991. Formula 3000 followed, with David winning but not landing a Formula One ride until he signed to be Williams' test driver. This turned into a race seat in 1994 when Ayrton Senna was killed. Starting with a top team has its advantages and David was a winner in 1995, ending up third overall. He moved to McLaren in 1996 and won the 1997 Australian Grand Prix to give the team its first win since 1993, going on to finish third that year and again in 1998. Despite winning at Silverstone and Spa in 1999 he slipped back to fourth overall.

TRACK NOTES

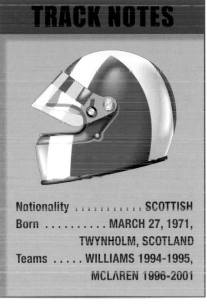

Nationality . . . . SCOTTISH
Born . . . . MARCH 27, 1971,
TWYNHOLM, SCOTLAND
Teams . . . . . WILLIAMS 1994-1995,
MCLAREN 1996-2001

CAREER RECORD

First Grand Prix	1994 SPANISH GP
Grand Prix starts	107
Grand Prix wins	9

1995 Portuguese GP, 1997 Australian GP, 1997 Italian GP, 1998 San Marino GP, 1999 British GP, 1999 Belgian GP, 2000 British GP, 2000 Monaco GP, 2000 French GP

Poles	10
Fastest laps	14
Points	294
Honours	1991 BRITISH

FORMULA THREE RUNNER-UP & WINNER OF MACAU GP, 1989 MCLAREN AUTOSPORT YOUNG DRIVER OF THE YEAR, 1989 BRITISH JUNIOR FORMULA FORD CHAMPION, 1988 SCOTTISH KART CHAMPION

NO DISTRACTIONS: David Coulthard's clearer focus paid dividends in 2000

WILLIAMS

BACK ON THE UP

Williams surprised everyone when its first year with BMW produced a third place in the Constructors' Cup. With Ralf Schumacher and Juan Pablo Montoya as drivers, the team hopes to gun for wins in 2001.

Williams has been in a trough since it lost its works Renault engine deal at the end of 1997 – the year of its last World Championship success. However, there's no doubt that the team is finding its way again and that its second year with works BMW engines could see the team challenging at the front again, after pulling itself to the top of the midfield pack to end last year's Constructor's Cup third overall.

The British press was upset last summer when it became clear that its new glory boy, Jenson Button, would not be kept on for a second season with Williams. He was, you see, just keeping the seat warm until former Williams test driver Juan Pablo Montoya returned from a title-winning sojourn in ChampCars. Ralf Schumacher was secure in the team's number-one seat, but Button was unable to hang on to his ride, even though a long-term retainer should see him as a Williams driver again in 2003 after a two-year stint at Benetton. So the media started writing stories that Sir Frank Williams' capacity for getting rid of top drivers or champions had struck again, Button joining the likes of Nigel Mansell and Damon Hill.

One of the key ingredients will be its Michelin tyres – and these don't come untried, with Williams having had a test team dedicated to the task of developing them, putting in enormous mileage through last year. Jorg Muller was the driver at the wheel, using the experience he had gained in 1998 when he performed a similar task for Williams in the development of the BMW engine that impressed so much in 2000. For this year, the second-generation BMW engine will be 20kg lighter than last year's, and smaller too.

IN CONTROL: Sir Frank Williams runs the team with a rod of iron, seeking success

Either Nigel Mansell or Nelson Piquet should have been crowned in 1986, but McLaren's Alain Prost stole past in the final round. Piquet made no mistake in 1987 though. Williams produced a car that was the class of the field in 1992 and Mansell roared to the title. Prost did likewise in 1993. Damon Hill could have made it a hat-trick in 1994, but Michael Schumacher muscled him out. Two years later, Hill got his rewards, with Jacques Villeneuve becoming the seventh Williams driver to be World Champion in 1997. Since then, with the loss of works Renault engines and designer Adrian Newey, Williams has taken a backwards step. But the team will rise again.

HEAD MAN: Technical director Patrick Head is optimistic about the season ahead in 2001, but has expressed concern that the team's tyre supplier – Michelin – will have to face up to a steep learning curve in its battle with rivals, Bridgestone

IN WITH A BANG

BMW spent the winter of 1999 saying that 2000 would be a learning year. Perhaps because of this, people didn't expect that much from Williams last year. And so everyone was shocked when Schumacher raced to third place behind the two Ferraris in the opening round at Melbourne. The McLarens had both retired, but this was a performance of great promise, especially as new-boy Button had run in the points until his engine failed in the closing laps. With both drivers in the points next time out at Interlagos, and again two races later at Silverstone, their season was full of promise. However, the FW22 was held back by performing poorly on low-grip tracks, but this improved markedly at the Hungarian Grand Prix when mid-wings and sidepod-mounted wings were introduced after being tried at Monaco. Schumacher responded by qualifying fourth and finishing fifth. He then went even better in Belgium and Italy, placing third each time. Button's finest moment was at Hockenheim, where he was made to start at the back of the grid and raced through to fourth place. Between them, their scores were enough to leave Williams a clear third in the Constructors' Cup.

FROM HUMBLE BEGINNINGS

Frank Williams was considered a bit of a joke in the Formula One paddock in the 1970s, as he never had any money and his cars ran at the back of the field. But then in 1977 he teamed up with Patrick Head to form the team we know today. Landing crucial sponsorship with Saudia financed their progress, with Clay Regazzoni scoring the team's first win in 1979. A year later, Alan Jones was World Champion. And this was just the beginning, as Keke Rosberg followed suit in 1982.

FOR THE RECORD

Country of origin	England
Team base	Grove, England
Date of formation	1968
Active years in Formula One	From 1973
Grands Prix contested	428
Wins	103
Pole positions	108
Fastest laps	111
Constructors' Cup victories	1980, 1981, 1986, 1987, 1992, 1993, 1994, 1996, 1997

DRIVERS + RESULTS 2000

Driver	Nationality	Races	Wins	Pts	Pos
Ralf Schumacher	German	17	0	24	5th
Jenson Button	English	17	0	12	8th

CAR SPECIFICATIONS

Sponsors	BMW, Compaq, Castrol, Nortel
Team principal	Frank Williams
Technical director	Patrick Head
Team manager	Dickie Stanford
Designers	Gavin Fisher and Geoff Willis
Chief engineer	James Robinson
Test driver	Mark Gene
Chassis	Williams FW23
Engine	BMW V10
Tyres	Michelin

RALF SCHUMACHER

READY TO WIN

Ralf Schumacher, BMW and Williams progressed better than people expected last year. Now, if everything goes according to plan, he should be looking towards scoring his first Grand Prix victory in 2001.

In a few short years, Ralf Schumacher has gone from Formula One rookie to part of the old guard. Not yet a winner, few doubt that he will become one if Williams and BMW can produce a better package. However, Ralf is on edge about the arrival of new team-mate Juan Pablo Montoya, a driver who took a break after being Williams' test driver in 1998 to win the ChampCar title in 1999. How they get on is going to be one of the talking-points of the year.

Ralf was in a win-win situation last year, as no-one expected much from Williams because of the arrival of BMW engines. This was a development year, yet there was Ralf finishing third in the opening race. Using his smooth speed, Ralf added a pair of thirds in the Belgian and Italian Grands Prix.

However, there was one blot on the landscape: his novice team-mate Jenson Button, who had the audacity to outqualify him as early as the second race at Interlagos, and then a further five more times into the bargain.

IN MICHAEL'S FOOTSTEPS

Everything that Ralf achieved in racing was always going to be compared with what Michael had achieved before him. So perhaps it was fortunate that there are six years between them, so the dust could settle. Ralf started in Formel Junior midway through 1992. He stayed on for a full season in 1993, finishing as runner-up. Moving to German Formula Three in 1994, Ralf was run by Willi Weber, the man behind Michael's career. A winner before the year was out, he ranked third, then went one better in 1995 when he was runner-up to Norberto Fontana.

Ralf's next move was to Japan to race in Formula Nippon, and three wins gave him the title. This landed him his Formula One break with Jordan, and Ralf surprised many people with his speed – maybe he was more than "just Michael's brother". Third place in Argentina was his best result, but his season was littered with accidents. His second year was more controlled, and he peaked with second at Spa-Francorchamps. Ralf moved to Williams in 1999 and impressed with his mature racing; second at Monza was his best result, but had his car not suffered a puncture, he could have won the European Grand Prix at the Nurburgring.

UNDER PRESSURE: Ralf found himself having to give his all to keep his team-mate Jenson Button behind him. This year he has Juan Pablo Montoya to be concerned about

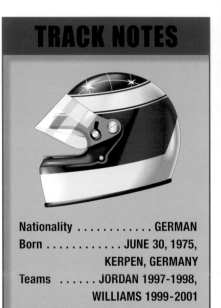

TRACK NOTES

Nationality	GERMAN
Born	JUNE 30, 1975, KERPEN, GERMANY
Teams	JORDAN 1997-1998, WILLIAMS 1999-2001

CAREER RECORD

First Grand Prix	1997 AUSTRALIAN GP
Grand Prix starts	66
Grand Prix wins	NONE
	(best result: second, 1998 Belgian GP & 1999 Italian GP)
Poles	NONE
Fastest laps	1
Points	86
Honours	1996 FORMULA NIPPON CHAMPION, 1995 GERMAN FORMULA THREE RUNNER-UP & MACAU GP WINNER, 1993 GERMAN FORMEL JUNIOR RUNNER-UP

JUAN PABLO MONTOYA

SOUTH AMERICAN FLIER

Juan Pablo Montoya is expected to make a major impact when he crosses over from ChampCars to fill Jenson Button's seat at Williams. The 1998 Formula 3000 champion is quick, but will he be hard enough?

TRACK NOTES

Nationality	COLOMBIAN
Born	SEPTEMBER 20, 1975, BOGOTA, COLOMBIA
Teams	WILLIAMS 2001

CAREER RECORD

First Grand Prix	2001 AUSTRALIAN GP
Grand Prix starts	NONE
Grand Prix wins	NONE
Poles	NONE
Fastest laps	NONE
Points	NONE
Honours	2000 INDY 500 WINNER, 1999 INDYCAR CHAMPION, 1998 FORMULA 3000 CHAMPION

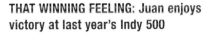

THAT WINNING FEELING: Juan enjoys victory at last year's Indy 500

Juan Pablo Montoya has many fans inside the sport, but he also has his critics, and among their ranks is none other than his new team-mate, Ralf Schumacher. So, this season is sure to be an interesting one at Williams. It comes down to Juan Pablo's perceived arrogance, and this is part of his character make-up that is unmistakable. Put simply, he is extraordinarily confident, rather in the mould of Ayrton Senna. His opinions of his ability come before him, and this is what was annoying Ralf before last season was out. However, Juan Pablo is very fast and a very brave racer, so why not?

The 25-year-old Colombian is determined to do better in Formula One than the last driver who crossed over from ChampCars,

Alessandro Zanardi, who failed to score a single point. That was also with Williams, but Juan Pablo has the advantage of having been test driver for Williams in 1998, so the team holds no surprises for him and he knows that team bosses Frank Williams and Patrick Head are fans of his skills. Formula One cars are certainly harder to drive to their full than ChampCars, but Juan Pablo's extreme focus is likely to work in his favour, to say nothing of his natural speed and outrageous car control.

A ROOKIE CHAMPION

A karting ace at home in Colombia, Juan Pablo raced in the USA in 1994, finishing third in the Barber Saab Pro-Series. Juan Pablo raced in British Formula Vauxhall in 1995, ending up third overall. He graduated to Formula Three in 1986, but suffered from

running a Mitsubishi engine when Mugens dominated, and ranked fifth. Juan Pablo raced in Formula 3000 in 1997, winning three times to be second overall. He joined Super Nova in 1998 and was champion after winning four of the 12 races to beat Nick Heidfeld to the title. He joined Chip Ganassi Racing in 1999 and became the first driver since Nigel Mansell to win the ChampCar title at the first attempt, racing to seven wins.

Last year, Ganassi swapped both chassis and engine, from Reynard to Lola and from Honda to Toyota. The speed was there, as shown by a handful of pole positions and wins at Milwaukee, Michigan and Gateway, but Juan Pablo's string of non-scores cost him dear and left him ninth in the final rankings. However, the highlight of his year came at the non-championship Indianapolis 500, a race he dominated to win.

BENETTON

LOOKING AHEAD

Benetton is a team that is anxious to reinvent itself. In come works engines from Renault, a new designer in the form of Mike Gascoyne and Formula One's hottest property, Jenson Button. Only time will tell, but it looks as though the team is back on track for Grand Prix success.

Benetton is a team that's looking to reinvent itself so that it can arrest the slide that started in 1996 following the departure of Michael Schumacher after winning the drivers' title with the English team in both 1994 and 1995. Indeed, Benetton won the Constructors' Cup for the one and only time in the second of those campaigns. Yet, apart from Gerhard Berger's surprise win in the 1997 German Grand Prix, Benetton hasn't won a race in the past five World Championships.

Now, with Renault returning as a partner for 2001 and beyond, bringing with it works engines that are likely to be more competitive than the Playlife-badged customer V10s the team used last year, the excuses are no longer there: success is expected. Works engines, a chassis tweaked by Gascoyne and a driver line-up of Button and Giancarlo Fisichella ought to be good enough to pick up the pieces on the odd days that Ferrari or McLaren trip up in the season ahead.

POWER TALKING: Pat Symonds runs the Benetton operation and knows the team inside-out

FOR THE RECORD

Country of origin	England
Team base	Enstone, England
Date of formation	1986
Active years in Formula One	From 1986
Grands Prix contested	344
Wins	27
Pole positions	16
Fastest laps	35
Constructors' Cup victories	1995

DRIVERS + RESULTS 2000

Driver	Nationality	Races	Wins	Pts	Pos
Giancarlo Fisichella	Italian	17	0	18	6th
Alexander Wurz	Austrian	17	0	0	N/A

CAR SPECIFICATIONS

Sponsors	Playlife, Mild Seven, Marconi, Korean Air
Team principal	Flavio Briatore
Team manager	Steve Nielsen
Technical director	Mike Gascoyne
Designers	Ben Agathangelou, Tim Densham and Chris Radage
Chief engineer	Pat Symonds
Test driver	Mark Webber
Chassis	Benetton B201
Engine	Renault V10
Tyres	Michelin

SILVER FOX: Flavio Briatore continues to push not only for success, but glamour in the pitlane too

A BATTLE WITHIN

Watch out for the battle for supremacy between Fisichella – back for his fourth year with Benetton – and Button. Such was Fisichella's position of favoritism within the team in 2000 that it seemed hard to imagine another driver being allowed a look-in. However, towards the end of last year, team boss Flavio Briatore started to be openly critical of his compatriot, suggesting that the opportunity presented to Button might be greater than it was to Benetton number-two Alexander Wurz last year. For example, Briatore said of Fisichella after qualifying at last year's United States Grand Prix: "Alex applied his mind and studied everything carefully before arriving at Indianapolis, while Giancarlo tried to rely on his talent which is no

substitute for hard work." Button himself is confident that he will become a Grand Prix winner with Benetton, with this breakthrough win for the 21-year-old coming either this season or next. After that, he has no idea for which team he will be racing, as Williams has a call on his services for 2003 and beyond.

Looking back at last year is not something that Benetton will wish to do – even though it overhauled the likes of Jordan who had been so much more competitive in 1999 – for their level of competitiveness was inconsistent. In a bid to establish themselves, the team effectively brought out a B-spec of their B200 model at the Hungarian GP in August, introducing major aerodynamic modifications including more obvious flip-ups in front of the rear wheels and swoopier rear bodywork.

Yet, although Wurz started scoring after that, Fisichella stopped doing so, never finding himself in a position to match the second place he claimed at Interlagos or the brace of third places at Monaco and Montreal. The team held on to fourth place in the Constructors' Cup, even though BAR matched their points tally.

FROM TOLEMAN TO TODAY

There is a blurring of history when people look back on Benetton's past for the team is listed as starting in 1986, yet it did so by taking over the Toleman team that had raced in Formula One since 1981. To confuse matters further, Benetton had previously been involved as a sponsor with Tyrrell, Alfa Romeo and then Toleman. Entered as Benetton from 1986, the highlight of the team's early years was Berger giving the team its first win in Mexico City. It took three more years before the next Benetton win, when Alessandro Nannini was handed victory at Suzuka after Ayrton Senna was disqualified following his title-settling clash with Alain Prost. Nelson Piquet then won the final two races in 1990, but it was the arrival of Michael Schumacher that proved to be Benetton's turning point. Although he scored his first win with Benetton in 1992, it wasn't until 1994 that it all came together and he won eight times to be champion. He went one better in 1995, winning nine races en route to his second title, with team-mate Johnny Herbert winning twice, but then the brain-drain opened and technical chief Ross Brawn and designer Rory Byrne followed him to Ferrari and the wins dried up.

GIANCARLO FISICHELLA

LOOKING TO RENAULT

Giancarlo Fisichella will be boosted by works engines this year, and will be hoping that this new-found Renault horsepower can put his flagging career back on track. Only a consistent season will help preserve his reputation.

Quick, but highly-strung would be one way of describing this pixie-like Roman. He's had the better of team-mate Alexander Wurz throughout their three-year spell at Benetton. However, he was very

THE WAITING GAME: Giancarlo waits around stoically in the endless testing between the Grands Prix

much Benetton's number one, as returning team-boss Flavio Briatore favoured him over Wurz. And this year it is Giancarlo who should be fearful of not receiving the team's best equipment, as Briatore seems to have taken a shine to his latest signing. In Jenson Button, Giancarlo has a team-mate who is inexperienced and isn't yet a Grand Prix winner, but he's a driver who is considered quick. So, if he keeps the English driver in his wake, his career will regain the momentum it has lost as Benetton has struggled without works engines for the past three years. Works horsepower from Renault and the challenge from within could provide just the spark to reignite the career of a driver to whom it all appeared to come so easily.

Giancarlo finished fifth in last year's opening race in Melbourne. With the McLarens having failed, he can't have fancied his chances next time out in Brazil, yet he ended up second after David Coulthard was disqualified. Reality struck and Benetton slipped to the midfield, but Giancarlo brightened his summer with third places in the Canadian and French Grands Prix. Then, as has so often been the case with Giancarlo, the points dried up. He should have scored at Hockenheim, but clashed with Michael Schumacher at the first corner, then a clutch problem cost him fourth at Monza.

EARLY GLORY

Giancarlo was one of the drivers on the international kart-racing scene who was tipped for future car-racing glory, and he showed why when he impressed in Formula Alfa Boxer in 1991 before finishing as runner-up in Italian Formula Three in 1993.

TRACK NOTES

Nationality . . . . ITALIAN
Born . . . . JANUARY 14, 1973,
ROME, ITALY
Teams . . . . MINARDI 1996,
JORDAN 1997,
BENETTON 1998-2001

CAREER RECORD

First Grand Prix 1996
AUSTRALIAN GP
Grand Prix starts 74
Grand Prix wins . . . . NONE
(best result: second, 1997 Belgian GP,
1998 Monaco GP, 1998 Canadian GP,
1999 Canadian GP, 2000 Brazilian GP)
Poles 1
Fastest laps 1
Points 67
Honours . . . . 1994 ITALIAN
FORMULA THREE CHAMPION &
MONACO FORMULA THREE GP
WINNER, 1991 EUROPEAN
KART RUNNER-UP

He followed this by winning the title in 1994 and the Monaco Formula Three race. A lack of money to advance in single-seaters saw him spend two years racing in touring cars for Alfa Romeo before Minardi snapped him up for a shot at Formula One in 1996. Giancarlo moved to Jordan in 1997, shining by leading at Hockenheim then finishing second at Spa-Francorchamps. A long-term management contract took him to Benetton in 1998. But, although a podium visitor every year since, he's never had a winning car beneath him.

JENSON BUTTON

THE SURPRISE OF 2000

Some of the sport's top names said his leap from Formula Three to Formula One with Williams last year was too large a step, but Jenson Button proved them wrong as he took to it like a duck to water. Armed with a year's experience, he's now with Benetton.

CAREER RECORD

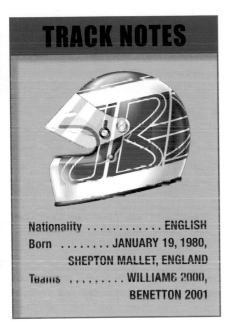

TRACK NOTES

Nationality . . . . ENGLISH
Born . . . . JANUARY 19, 1980,
SHEPTON MALLET, ENGLAND
Teams . . . . WILLIAMS 2000,
BENETTON 2001

First Grand Prix 2000	
AUSTRALIAN GP	
Grand Prix starts 17	
Grand Prix wins . . . . NONE	
(best result: fourth, 2000 German GP)	
Poles . . . . None	
Fastest laps . . . . None	
Points 12	
Honours . . . . 1999 MACAU	

FORMULA THREE RUNNER-UP,
1998 FORMULA FORD FESTIVAL
WINNER & BRITISH FORMULA
FORD CHAMPION, 1998 McLAREN
AUTOSPORT BRDC YOUNG DRIVER,
1997 EUROPEAN SUPER A
KARTING CHAMPION, 1991 BRITISH
CADET KART CHAMPION

The fifth youngest driver ever to have raced in Formula One, Jenson Button appeared not to find this a problem. After all, despite having little pre-season testing, having only beaten Bruno Junqueira to the drive at the 11th hour, Jenson was heading for points on his debut until his engine seized. To show that this was no fluke, he outqualified team-mate Ralf Schumacher next time out at Interlagos, and raced on to his first point. Thus a star was born.

One of the most astounding aspects of Jenson's first season is that he made fewer mistakes than any other driver. A German journalist kept a tally of how many times drivers spun, ran off the circuit or crashed during the season, and the 20-year-old novice was the least accident-prone of all,

proving the doubters wrong. That he scored on six occasions, peaking with fourth in the German Grand Prix, showed that not only did he keep the car on the island and pointing in the right direction, but that he was on the pace too.

Looking to the season ahead, he has swapped a Williams-BMW for a Benetton-Renault, making way for ChampCar ace Juan Pablo Montoya to race for Williams, so he'll have to cope with a new team, a new chassis and a new engine. However, people say Williams isn't the most forgiving environment in which to spend one's rookie season and yet Jenson thrived, so he's tougher than many reckoned. Indeed, despite turning 21 this March, Jenson seems wise beyond his years, and this season is his chance to show that his rookie form was no flash in the pan. Williams will watch with interest, as it still has Jenson on a long-term contract and may call him back for 2003.

RACING IS IN HIS BLOOD

Jenson's family is steeped in motorsport, as his father John was a leading rallycross driver in the 1970s. Jenson was duly racing karts as soon as he was old enough, winning the British Cadet title at the age of 11. He then shone in the junior classes, before winning the European Super A title in 1997. A stunning first season in Formula Ford followed when Jenson not only won the British Championship, but also scooped the prestigious Formula Ford Festival. Pole position for his first Formula Three race in 1999 showed that he was one to watch, and

he wore the victor's garland third time out and went on to finish the year third overall. Initially he considered a second year in Formula Three or one in Formula 3000.

REASON TO SMILE: Jenson Button was predicted by many of the sport's insiders to stumble in 2000. He did quite the reverse and goes to Benetton with a huge reputation

BRITISH AMERICAN RACING

MOVING FORWARD

It was essential that BAR scored championship points in its second season – which it did – but it wants more in 2001, and with Jacques Villeneuve and a recharged Olivier Panis on its driving staff, it has its best chance yet.

TEAM TALK: Designer Malcolm Oastler and team principal Craig Pollock discuss the best way forward. Expect further progress in BAR's third season

THE VIPS

CRAIG POLLOCK

Craig was a ski instructor when he met Jacques Villeneuve. Moving into marketing, he met up again with Jacques who was racing in Japan, and agreed to manage his racing career. This brought him to Formula One and Craig soon decided to establish his own team, BAR, buying out Tyrrell's World Championship entry to do so.

ADRIAN REYNARD

Adrian began his career by racing sprint motorbikes. Then he raced single-seaters, building his own Formula Ford. That was in 1972, and his company blossomed, with Reynard cars winning titles up to F3000 and ChampCar level. Adrian was a founding partner of BAR.

QUICK OFF THE MARK

Villeneuve set the ball rolling when he finished fourth in the first race of last year, at Melbourne, instantly expunging BAR's scoreless maiden season. That team-mate Ricardo Zonta was also in the points, finishing sixth, was the icing on the cake, showing from the outset that the team was going to be more of a factor with its works Honda engines than it had been in 1999.

Villeneuve produced a series of scorching starts, with his getaway from sixth on the grid in the Canadian Grand Prix to run third – later second – perhaps his best. Yet, none led to that longed-for first visit to a Grand Prix podium, with Villeneuve having to settle for three further fourth places, at Magny-Cours, at the A1-Ring and at Indianapolis. If these were the high points, then a collision with Zonta during the German Grand Prix was the nadir. Villeneuve took the opportunity to tell the media that he had no time for his

Craig Pollock is the man who created British American Racing, who came up with the idea, found the backing from British American Tobacco to make it happen, bought out Tyrrell's entry to the World Championship and convinced his former protégé Villeneuve to quit Williams and join him. However, cracks started to appear last year when BAT said that it wasn't satisfied with BAR's results. ChampCar team boss

Barry Green was then contacted about taking over at the helm, being well known by BAT as it backs his team with its Kool brand. He was also an obvious choice as he ran the team's number one Jacques Villeneuve in Toyota Atlantic in 1993, then in ChampCars in 1994 and 1995. However, the approach came to nothing and Green will remain in ChampCars rather than becoming BAR's, with Pollock staying on as BAR's chairman.

Brazilian team-mate, as "he has gone off in every other race because he drives over his limit". Zonta knew then that his spell with BAR wouldn't last for a third year but, ironically, he proceeded to drive with greater maturity to score points at Monza and Indianapolis. That he was still racing was testament to his good fortune, as he'd survived massive accidents when parts broke in testing at Silverstone and at Monza. His upturn in form and late-season scores from Villeneuve left BAR level on points with Benetton for fourth place in the Constructors' Cup, but they were classified fifth as Benetton had scored a third to BAR's best result of fourth.

While Zonta had to look elsewhere for his employment for this year, Villeneuve talked of doing likewise for 2002 if BAR doesn't raise its game further. And that means putting him in a car that offers him a chance of winning rather than being a second a lap off the pace. Also keen for improved performance in 2001 is engine supplier Honda, with internal pressures making it essential that they start to

FOR THE RECORD

Country of origin	England
Team base	Brackley, England
Date of formation	1998
Active years in Formula One	From 1999
Grands Prix contested	33
Wins	NONE
Pole positions	NONE
Fastest laps	NONE

DRIVERS + RESULTS 2000

Driver	Nationality	Races	Wins	Pts	Pos
Jacques Villeneuve	Canadian	17	0	17	7th
Ricardo Zonta	Brazilian	17	0	3	14th

CAR SPECIFICATIONS

Sponsors	British American Tobacco, Teleglobe
Team principal	Craig Pollock
Technical director	Adrian Reynard
Team manager	Ron Meadows
Designer	Malcolm Oastler
Chief engineer	Jock Clear
Test driver	Darren Manning
Chassis	BAR 003
Engine	Honda V10
Tyres	Bridgestone

POWER PLAYER: Adrian Reynard has had his disagreements with Craig Pollock but both really want BAR to succeed

see some return on their investment. In addition, news broke in Suzuka last year that Honda was considering buying out BAT's share of the team and turning it into a works Honda team to take on Toyota head-on in 2002. This is no longer the case, though Honda came very close to launching a works team for 2000 – but the project folded when its front man Harvey Postlethwaite died in 1999.

A TROUBLED START

BAR ruffled a few feathers in 1998 as it geared up for its arrival in Formula One in 1999. Founding partner Adrian Reynard told anyone who cared to listen that the team would win on its debut, as Reynard cars had in Formula Three, Formula 3000 and ChampCars. Pollock tried to tone down these boasts, but still reckoned that the team would win at least once. Armed with a healthy budget from BAT and Villeneuve and rookie Zonta in the race seats, BAR came away with egg on its face as Villeneuve not only failed to win, but failed even to score. Indeed, he didn't even finish a race until the Belgian Grand Prix at the end of August. His best finish was an eighth place at Monza, matched by Zonta at the Nurburgring. Mika Salo stood in for Zonta when the Brazilian damaged tendons in his right foot, and produced the team's top result: seventh at Imola.

JACQUES VILLENEUVE

THIRD TIME LUCKY?

Jacques Villeneuve is aching for BAR to succeed. If it doesn't, he'll be taking his talents to one of the established teams, as three years with an underachieving team would dull the lust for racing of even this racer's racer.

This will be Jacques Villeneuve's third year with BAR, the team set up by his friend and former manager Craig Pollock. Yet, for all its financial clout, the team has yet to deliver the goods. Jacques, on the other hand, has never shown himself to be less than a committed driver, someone who will score points every time he's given a car capable of doing the job. He is a 100% sort of guy. Well, in the cockpit at least, as his dislike of the media and sponsorship duties shows no sign of abating.

After the disappointment of scoring no points at all in BAR's maiden season, Jacques finished fourth in the opening race. Using a Honda works engine, Jacques enjoyed power aplenty, but the BAR chassis wasn't the class of the field and so progress was limited. He raced to a further pair of fourth places at Magny-Cours and the A1-Ring. Then he somehow avoided the first-lap carnage at Monza to run a clear third, only to retire with electrical failure. However, he bounced back with fourth at Indianapolis and fifth at Sepang, but his desire to win again is well known.

SON OF A RACER

Jacques took the route of so many sons of racing fathers when he followed his late father Gilles into the sport. Starting in 1989, he improved over a three-year spell in Italian Formula Three, to finish sixth overall in 1991. Jacques was runner-up in the Japanese Formula Three series in 1992, but it was the fact that he met up with his former school-teacher Pollock that boosted his career, as Craig found the money for him to progress to the North American Toyota Atlantic Championship. Third overall and rookie of the year, he did enough to move into Champ Cars. Rookie of the year in 1994, finishing second in the Indy 500, he improved from sixth overall to first in 1995 and Bernie Ecclestone orchestrated his move to Formula One for 1996.

Team-mate to Damon Hill at Williams, he won four times to be second overall. As team number one in 1997, Jacques won seven times to take the title battle with Michael Schumacher to the final round, surviving an assault from the German to take the title. However, the loss of works Renault engines in 1998 left Williams struggling and Jacques had to make do with a pair of thirds. Then he joined Pollock at BAR in 1999, scoring not a single point.

TRACK NOTES

Nationality .... CANADIAN
Born .... APRIL 9, 1971,
   ST JEAN-SUR-RICHELIEU, CANADA
Teams ..... WILLIAMS 1996-1998,
   BAR 1999-2001

CAREER RECORD

First Grand Prix 1996
   AUSTRALIAN GP
Grand Prix starts 82
Grand Prix wins 11
   1996 European GP, 1996 British GP,
   1996 Hungarian GP,
   1996 Portuguese GP,
   1997 Brazilian GP,
   1997 Argentinian GP,
   1997 Spanish GP, 1997 British GP,
   1997 Hungarian GP,
   1997 Austrian GP,
   1997 Luxembourg GP
Poles 13
Fastest laps 9
Points 197
Honours .... 1997 WORLD
   CHAMPION, 1996 FORMULA ONE
   RUNNER-UP, 1995 INDYCAR
   CHAMPION, 1994 INDYCAR ROOKIE
   OF THE YEAR, 1993 TOYOTA
   ATLANTIC ROOKIE OF THE YEAR,
   1992 JAPANESE FORMULA
   THREE RUNNER-UP

JACQUES THE LAD: No-one appeared to try harder than Jacques in 2000. The signs are that BAR will give him a car to match his talents

OLIVIER PANIS

BACK IN THE DRIVING SEAT

A year spent as test driver for McLaren has rejuvenated Olivier Panis, proving that he can be as quick as Hakkinen and Coulthard. Now, teamed up with Jacques Villeneuve at BAR, he is ready to impress again.

TRACK NOTES

Nationality .... FRENCH
Born .... 2 SEPTEMBER 1966, LYONS, FRANCE
Teams .. LIGIER/PROST 1994-1999, BAR 2001

CAREER RECORD

First Grand Prix .... 1994 BRAZILIAN GP
Grand Prix starts 91
Grand Prix wins 1
1996 Monaco GP
Poles .... NONE
Fastest laps .... NONE
Points 56
Honours .... 1993 FORMULA 3000 CHAMPION, 1991 FRENCH FORMULA THREE RUNNER-UP, 1989 FRENCH FORMULA RENAULT CHAMPION

Getting into Formula One is harder than ever. However, one thing that is harder still is to leave Formula One and find a way back in: step forward Olivier Panis. Martin Brundle and Derek Warwick both dropped out and returned, but they did so after spending their sabbatical racing sportscars. Olivier, on the other hand, last raced in the 1999 Japanese Grand Prix.

Dropped by Prost after six years, it looked as though that was the last we would see of Olivier. However, McLaren respects experience and signed Olivier in place of the up-and-coming test drivers it had used previously. They wanted a driver who could accurately relate what was happening to the car, taking the pressure off Hakkinen and Coulthard in tests. Olivier did everything that McLaren could have wished, and they were sad when he signed with BAR for a return to racing. However, that's not the end of experienced test drivers, with McLaren replacing Olivier with Alexander Wurz and Jordan snapping up Ricardo Zonta. Olivier has started a trend.

SIX YEARS IN ONE TEAM

Olivier's career was launched when he won a Formula Renault scholarship in 1988. The French title followed in 1989, and the French Formula Three title in 1991. Winning the Formula 3000 Championship in 1993 helped Olivier attract the attention of Ligier, who signed him for 1994. He finished 15 of the 16 Grands Prix that year, even outscoring his team-mate Eric Bernard. A surprise second place came his way in the 1995 Australian Grand Prix, but his third year was a step backwards, apart from one race at

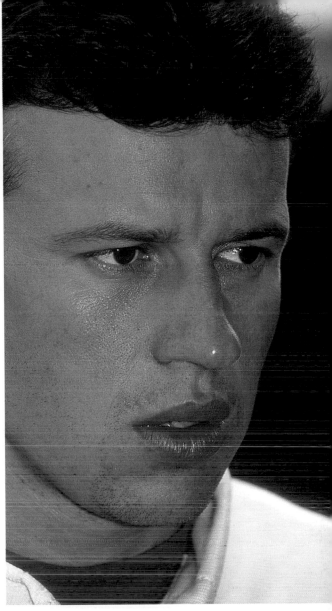

RARING TO GO: A season as test driver has left Olivier ultra-keen to go racing again

Monaco that he won against all the odds in the wet.

Olivier's suspension failed at Montreal in 1997 and he broke both legs in the crash that resulted. Amazingly, he was racing again within three months, regretting only that the accident had curtailed a year in which he had a good chassis, a strong engine from Mugen and durable tyres from Bridgestone, as shown by a third place in Brazil and running second in Argentina. Fourth in the wet at Monaco was followed by second in Spain, but then came that race in Canada...

All hope of progress in 1998 was hampered by an experimental gearbox, and his best result was ninth in the opening race. With no other options, Olivier re-signed for 1999, but his campaign produced only two sixth places and it ended with Olivier being dropped.

JORDAN

RESULTS REQUIRED

Jordan started last year on a high, having finished 1999 third overall, but slumped to finish sixth. The winter has been spent trying to rediscover its speed, and certainly some reliability, for what is a critical season.

The landing of a works-engine deal seems to have been the central tenet of Jordan's existence since it burst on to the Formula One scene in 1991. Thus an air of satisfaction settled over the team midway through last year when it landed a deal for this year to race with works Honda engines. However, voices within Honda have been heard to say that unless "tangible results" are recorded, they will withdraw again. So, both Jordan and BAR had better do everything within their power to ensure their futures with an engine supplier that grew accustomed to Constructors' Cup-winning success during its days with Williams (in 1986 and 1987) and McLaren (from 1988 to 1991).

LIKE CLOCKWORK: The Buzzin' Hornets do their stuff as Jarno Trulli calls in for a pitstop in 2000

FOR THE RECORD

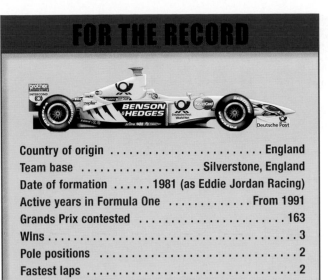

Country of origin	England
Team base	Silverstone, England
Date of formation	1981 (as Eddie Jordan Racing)
Active years in Formula One	From 1991
Grands Prix contested	163
Wins	3
Pole positions	2
Fastest laps	2

DRIVERS + RESULTS 2000

Driver	Nationality	Races	Wins	Pts	Pos
Heinz-Harald Frentzen	German	17	0	11	9th
Jarno Trulli	Italian	17	0	6	10th

CAR SPECIFICATIONS

Sponsors	Benson & Hedges, Deutsche Post, Master Card
Team principal	Eddie Jordan
Team manager	Trevor Foster
Designer	Eghbal Hamidy
Chief engineer	David Brown
Test driver	Ricardo Zonta
Chassis	Jordan EJ11
Engine	Honda V10
Tyres	Bridgestone

THE BOSS: Eddie Jordan watches on, hoping for a return to winning after a disappointing 2000 campaign dropped the team to sixth overall

Also new to Jordan for the season ahead is aerodynamicist Eghbal Hamidy, who was drafted in from Arrows to replace the outgoing Mike Gascoyne. However, his arrival was delayed by his former employers, meaning that his involvement in the design of the EJ11 wasn't as great as it could have been. Former Williams and McLaren engineer David Brown has joined to run Frentzen's car.

A YEAR OF FRUSTRATION

Heinz-Harald Frentzen became a firm favourite with Eddie Jordan when he won twice for the "Buzzin' Hornets" in 1999. However, there was never an opportunity for the German to repeat the feat last year. In fact, he managed to finish just six times as transmission problems laid the team low time and again. Jarno Trulli was expected to be a more competitive team-mate than Damon Hill had been in 1999, and so the Italian proved when the equipment allowed him to, with some impressive drives – including him claiming a front-row starting slot at Monaco. Indeed, Jordan was the only team to break the domination of the front row by Ferrari and McLaren. However, his gearbox failed when he was running second ahead of Coulthard's McLaren. The fact that leader Michael Schumacher then broke his car and handed victory to Coulthard was all the more galling, and Frentzen crashing out of second in the closing laps made it even worse. Look at the difference those 14 potential points would have made to Jordan's end-of-year position.

However, both Frentzen and Trulli are back for more, while the signing of Ricardo Zonta as test driver emphasizes how Jordan is getting serious, thanks to the input of backing from Honda. Of course, the Brazilian comes armed with two years of experience, and one of racing with Honda engines in his second season with BAR last year, but he also knows Jordan, having tested for them after he won the Formula 3000 title in 1997.

A DREAM BEGINNING

Eddie Jordan started his involvement in racing as a driver of some repute. But he reckoned that his skills would be best used running cars for others. And thus he set up a Formula Three outfit that ran the likes of Martin Brundle and Johnny Herbert. After title-winning success in Formula 3000 with Jean Alesi, this ambitious Irishman took the biggest gamble of his life and had a tilt at Formula One, arriving in 1991 with a sleek new car and drivers Andrea de Cesaris and Bertrand Gachot. Fifth overall that first year, Jordan took a wrong turn by signing for Yamaha works engines in 1992, but the team's performance chart turned upwards again in 1994.

Then in 1995 both Rubens Barrichello and Eddie Irvine made it to the podium at the Canadian Grand Prix. The next proud moment came in 1997 when Ralf Schumacher and Giancarlo Fisichella displayed great speed for the team. But its day of days came at the trouble-torn Belgian Grand Prix of 1998 when Damon Hill gave Jordan its first win, followed across the line by Ralf. Fourth overall that year, Jordan won twice through Frentzen in 1999 to rise to third overall and set their sights on the big two of Ferrari and McLaren.

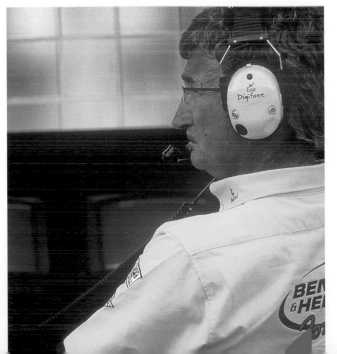

HEINZ-HARALD FRENTZEN

ANXIOUS TO BOUNCE BACK

After the heady success of 1999 with Jordan, Heinz-Harald ended last year frustrated following retirement after retirement, so he will be hoping that new Honda engines will help him back to the front in 2001.

Heinz-Harald Frentzen hoped for great things last year. He knew that an improvement on his third place in the 1999 drivers' championship was unlikely unless Michael Schumacher broke a leg again, but he hoped to be thereabouts. However, having a car that failed to carry him to the finish in 11 of the 17 Grands Prix helped not at all. Worse than that, the car wasn't always that competitive before it broke. A pair of thirds at Interlagos and Indianapolis was a poor substitute for the pair of wins he'd scored in 1999.

Added to Heinz-Harald's disappointment was the fact that team-mate Jarno Trulli outqualified him on eight occasions, and that will have rankled with a driver who had grown accustomed to being the top gun at Jordan.

The lowest points of Heinz-Harald's season came when he angered David Coulthard after they spoiled each other's qualifying runs at the Belgian Grand Prix. The problem resurfaced when he un-intentionally repeated the misdemeanour at Monza, but they patched up their differences. Then, the following day, Heinz-Harald's season went lower still when he triggered the first-lap accident that led to the death of a marshal, taking out not only Trulli, but also Barrichello and Coulthard. However, Heinz-Harald has toughened up since all wasn't going well for him at Williams, and this season is his chance to show that he really is one of the sport's very best.

THE EASTERN ROUTE

Heinz-Harald was national karting champion before he moved up to car racing, starting with FF2000 in 1986. Advancing to the all-new Formula Opel category in 1988, he became German champion and beat Mika Hakkinen in the final two European rounds. Equal second with Michael Schumacher in German Formula Three in 1989, he graduated to Formula 3000 in 1990, also racing for the Mercedes sportscar team. Heinz-Harald moved to Japanese Formula 3000 in 1992, enjoying two strong years before being snapped up to drive for Sauber in Formula One in 1994. On the pace immediately, he became the team's favourite, and his best result in his three years with the Swiss team was third at Monza in 1995. Heinz-Harald moved to Williams in 1997 and won at Imola, but was overshadowed by team-mate Jacques Villeneuve who won seven times. His move to Jordan in 1999 worked better and he thrived on the more personable atmosphere, showing his old skills to win twice, at Magny-Cours and Monza, to rank third overall.

WHY THE LONG FACE?: Heinz-Harald had a bad time in 2000 and is looking for an upturn

TRACK NOTES

Nationality	GERMAN
Born	MAY 18, 1967, MOENCHENGLADBACH, GERMANY
Teams	SAUBER 1994-1996, WILLIAMS 1997-1998, JORDAN 1999-2001

CAREER RECORD

First Grand Prix	1994 BRAZILIAN GP
Grand Prix starts	114
Grand Prix wins	3
	1997 San Marino GP, 1999 French GP, 1999 Italian GP
Poles	2
Fastest laps	6
Points	154
Honours	1989 GERMAN FORMULA THREE RUNNER-UP, 1988 GERMAN FORMULA OPEL CHAMPION, 1984 GERMAN JUNIOR KARTING CHAMPION

JARNO TRULLI

READY TO BLOSSOM

Jarno Trulli has always been seen as a potential Grand Prix winner since he burst into Formula One. With this in mind, he must be praying that Jordan and Honda can offer him a package competitive enough to remove that tag in 2001.

TRACK NOTES

Nationality	ITALIAN
Born	JULY 13, 1974, PESCARA, ITALY
Teams	MINARDI 1997, PROST 1997-1999, JORDAN 2000-2001

CAREER RECORD

First Grand Prix	1997 AUSTRALIAN GP
Grand Prix starts	63
Grand Prix wins	NONE
(best result: second, 1999 European GP)	
Poles	NONE
Fastest laps	NONE
Points	17
Honours	1996 GERMAN FORMULA THREE CHAMPION, 1994 WORLD KARTING CHAMPION

LOOKING AHEAD: Jarno Trulli showed great flashes of speed in 2000, but will be hoping to land a top result this time around

Jarno Trulli remains a great talent yet to blossom. People thought that last year, his first with Jordan, would signal the start of his establishment in the top flight of Formula One stars. Yet, the mechanical frailty of his car and its fluctuating competitiveness meant that he had to satisfy himself with flashes of promise rather than a constant flow.

There's no doubting that this self-assured Italian settled in quickly at Jordan, as he soon started to exert pressure on his team-mate Heinz-Harald Frentzen.

When Jarno qualified on the front row at Monaco he laid down a marker, but his run in second ended with gearbox failure. He also qualified on the front row at Spa-Francorchamps, but fourth at Interlagos was his best result all year. Jarno had been set for third at Hockenheim, but suffered a stop/go penalty for allegedly passing Rubens Barrichello under yellow flags as the Ferrari driver emerged from the pits. Then he was fourth on the first lap at Monza, but was taken out in an accident triggered by his team-mate. He was then tipped out of the Belgian Grand Prix by Jenson Button and was angered further when Button touched his car and gave it a puncture during the United States Grand Prix.

A KARTING SUPERSTAR

In the ultra-competitive world of international karting, Jarno established himself as the driver to beat. After landing his first national title at the age of 14, he went on to claim the first of his two world titles at 17 in 1991. Trulli was also in the top three, and he achieved this feat on four more occasions. So it came as little surprise when his talents were noticed. This happened in 1995 when he was launched into Formula Three by Benetton boss Flavio Briatore, entering the German series halfway through the year. Incredibly, he was a winner even before the championship year was out, ranking fourth overall.

Staying in Germany in 1996, Jarno raced to the title and pronounced himself ready for Formula One. No Formula 3000 would be necessary and so he clinched an eleventh-hour deal to race for Minardi for the 1997 season, less than two years after his car-racing debut. Then Olivier Panis broke his legs in Canada and Jarno moved across to Prost. He impressed with fourth place at Hockenheim, then shocked everybody by leading the Austrian Grand Prix. A full-time ride with Prost produced little in 1998 and 1999 as the car wasn't competitive, but he'd done enough to sign for Jordan for the 2000 season.

SAUBER

A TEAM FOR YOUNG GUNS

It's all change at Sauber for 2001 with last year's drivers Diniz and Salo being replaced by German young gun Nick Heidfeld and considerably younger gun Kimi Raikkonen, the least experienced driver ever in Formula One.

Sauber is a team desperate to give itself an image, for it has been almost invisible over the past few seasons, something that's rather difficult on a grid of just 11 teams. So, with two young drivers taking the place of two experienced ones, it is hoping that they will propel the team into territories new. Certainly, the signing of Kimi Raikkonen, a driver with just 23 car races to his name, will attract press coverage like

SWISS PRECISION: The Sauber mechanics give Mika Salo's car the once-over during practice for last year's Australian Grand Prix at Melbourne

never before. Heidfeld, too, will be anxious to rediscover the form that took him to the Formula 3000 title in 1999, and which was somewhat suppressed at Prost last year. Whether their potential speed can make up for their lack of experience remains to be seen.

There have been personnel shake-ups as well, as Willy Rampf has taken charge of Sauber's design team, taking over from the long-serving Leo Ress who had been with the team since its arrival in Formula One in 1993.

Other than that, Sauber will race on with ex-works Ferrari engines. However, perhaps its technical progress will continue to be restricted by patriot Peter Sauber's decision to keep the team in rural Switzerland rather than relocate to Formula One's equivalent of California's "Silicon Valley" around London, thus leading to a turnover of technical staff.

A FALSE START

Sauber suffered a dual setback in the first two rounds. Firstly, Mika Salo was disqualified from sixth place at Melbourne, as his front wing was marginally outside its regulation parameters. This was infuriating for the Swiss team, but at least their new signing had been in there fighting with the likes of

THE VIPS

PETER SAUBER

This cigar-smoking Swiss team boss was a racer himself before he started running a sportscar team in 1970. Success was slow to follow, but he guided Mercedes to World Championship glory in 1989 and 1990 before Mercedes helped him enter Formula One. He has been a sole operator since 1995.

BEAT ZEHNDER

Sauber's team manager is a long-time team member, having been a mechanic back in the late 1980s when Sauber ran Mercedes' sportscars. He oversaw their preparation for their break into Formula One in 1992 and has been Sauber's team manager since 1994.

team failed to move forward as much as expected, with its progress interrupted when Karl Wendlinger crashed at Monaco and fell into a coma. Mercedes elected to supply its engines to McLaren in 1995, with Sauber using customer Ford engines instead, and Heinz-Harald Frentzen becoming the team's favourite as he raced to third place in the Italian Grand Prix. Johnny Herbert joined him in 1996, scoring a surprise third at Monaco, but the team was entrenched in the midfield, where it has remained ever since. A deal to run the previous year's Ferrari engines was struck for 1997, these badged as Petronas engines in deference to Sauber's Malaysian sponsor. Herbert collected a third place at the Hungaroring, but the arrival of Jean Alesi in 1998 saw Herbert fall from favour. Alesi qualified second in a topsy-turvy session at the A1-Ring and then collected a third in the Belgian Grand Prix, but elected to move on after a poor 1999 season.

REASON TO SMILE: Strong form in winter testing has given Peter Sauber a rare excuse to smile, with both Heidfeld and Raikkonen showing an extremely useful turn of speed

FOR THE RECORD

Country of origin . . . . Switzerland
Team base . . . . Hinwil, Switzerland
Date of formation 1970
Active years in Formula One . . . . From 1993
Grands Prix contested 130
Wins . . . . NONE
Pole positions . . . . NONE
Fastest laps . . . . NONE

BAR, Williams and Benetton. Of more concern was what happened next time out at the Brazilian Grand Prix when rear-wing failures in practice forced the team to take the decision to withdraw the cars from the event. Salo bounced back to be sixth next time out, at Imola, but his season was to be a typical Sauber one of usually finishing just outside the points. Indeed, team-mate Pedro Diniz had six top-10 finishes but unfortunately not one in those all-important first six places.

Salo always goes well at Monaco and he duly obliged with fifth place – a result he matched in the German Grand Prix. But, all too often, the team was invisible, its lack of development budget seeing it lose ground as the year progressed. It appeared, too, that perhaps Salo was backing off, safe in the knowledge that he was heading off to Toyota in 2001, as Diniz was ever closer to his pace. Certainly, the Brazilian was outqualified less frequently by the Finn than he had been in 1998 when they were team-mates at Arrows.

AN UNUSUAL PAST

Sauber is alone among the Formula One teams in that its roots are in sportscar racing rather than single-seaters. Indeed, Sauber didn't even run a team in Formula Three or Formula 3000 before making its move into Formula One. After helping Mercedes win the Le Mans 24 Hours in 1989, Sauber arrived in Formula One with Mercedes-financed Ilmor engines in 1993, with JJ Lehto giving them points on their debut. Despite having works Mercedes engines in 1994, the

DRIVERS + RESULTS 2000

Driver	Nationality	Races	Wins	Pts	Pos
Pedro Diniz	Brazilian	17	0	0	N/A
Mika Salo	Finnish	17	0	6	10th

CAR SPECIFICATIONS

Sponsors . . . . Red Bull, Petronas Malaysia
Team principal . . . . Peter Sauber
Team manager . . . . Beat Zehnder
Designer . . . . Willy Rampf
Chief engineer: . . . . Gabriele delli Colli
Test driver . . . . tba
Chassis . . . . Sauber C20
Engine . . . . Petronas Ferrari V10
Tyres . . . . Bridgestone

NICK HEIDFELD

TIME FOR A CHANGE

Nick Heidfeld deserves a break in 2001. Life at the struggling Prost team was difficult last year, but he matched the experienced Jean Alesi. A move to the more competitive Sauber team should offer more of a chance to shine.

TRACK NOTES

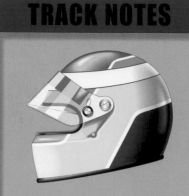

Nationality . . . . GERMAN
Born . . . . MAY 10, 1977,
MOENCHENGLADBACH, GERMANY
Teams . . . . PROST 2000,
SAUBER 2001

CAREER RECORD

First Grand Prix 2000
AUSTRALIAN GP
Starts 17
Wins . . . . NONE
(best result: eighth, 2000 Monaco GP)
Pole positions . . . . NONE
Fastest laps . . . . NONE
Points . . . . NONE
Honours . . . . 1999 FORMULA
3000 CHAMPION; 1998 FORMULA
3000 RUNNER-UP; 1997 GERMAN
FORMULA THREE CHAMPION;
1995 GERMAN FORMULA
FORD RUNNER-UP; 1994 GERMAN
FF1600 CHAMPION

It's amazing how quickly a driver's burgeoning reputation can be forgotten. After all, Nick Heidfeld almost did the impossible last year when he appeared to be more invisible having landed a Grand Prix ride than he had been before... So, you could say that life at Prost did him no more favours than his previous testing mileage with McLaren, especially as his car was seldom still running when the chequered flag fell. But his season with the French team did one thing: it compared him to Jean Alesi. That the 23-year-old German wasn't blown into the weeds by the most experienced driver racing in Formula One today speaks volumes for his ability behind the wheel. The lack of competitiveness of the Prost chassis and, especially, its Peugeot engine meant that Nick was seldom able to shine. Indeed, neither he nor Alesi was able to get in among the points all year.

THE POWER OF THOUGHT: Nick Heidfeld worked hard with no reward at Prost. He wants this year to be different

His move to Sauber won't necessarily cast him into the limelight, but he will be elevated to the position of a team leader, which is no small feat for a driver starting his second season in the World Championship. Whether Sauber can produce a better car than it did in 2000 remains to be seen, but Nick should enjoy having a more reliable and infinitely more powerful car beneath him, which will enable him to show TV audiences that he wasn't a champion in Formula Three and Formula 3000 for nothing.

QUICK FROM THE OUTSET

Nick starred in karting before progressing to Formula Ford at the age of 17. He was runner-up in the German championship the following year. However, it was in Formula Three that he made his name in 1996. Driving for Bertram Schafer Racing, Nick came on strong to win three races in succession to end up third overall in a season dominated by Jarno Trulli.

Nick went better still in 1997 to win a tight battle with Timo Scheider to be crowned champion. This helped him land the support of Mercedes and led to a Formula 3000 ride with the McLaren junior team for 1998. He won three of the 12 races, but lost out to Juan Pablo Montoya who won four. Despite his test seat with McLaren having given him useful Formula One mileage, no team wanted him for 1999, so Nick stayed on for a second season of Formula 3000, winning the title in style.

KIMI RAIKKONEN

THE LEAST EXPERIENCED YET

People said last year that Jenson Button was too inexperienced to tackle Formula One and succeed, and he proved them wrong. Now we have Kimi Raikkonen, who makes Button seem like the old man of the hills.

Jenson Button jumped from Formula Three to Formula One and made it, matching a wise approach to his obvious speed. For Kimi Raikkonen, he too is making a massive jump. But he's leaping onto the Grand Prix scene from a level further away, from Formula Renault, the category beneath Formula Three. And his first Grand Prix start will be only his 24th car racing start, this being the number of races that many drivers manage in their first season of car racing, with Formula One merely a dream that could be at least four years away.

Sauber tested the 21-year-old Finn twice last year, and Peter Sauber was so impressed at the way that he outpaced the team's test driver Enrique Bernoldi – a driver of repute in Formula 3000 – that he snapped him up for 2001.

Amazingly, the Australian GP will be only Kimi's 24th car race since stepping up from karts. And that's 21 races fewer than Button had to his name at the start of last season. The Sauber won't be as competitive a tool as the Williams was for Button last year, but

look for Kimi's sideways style and all-out attacking attitude.

Kimi and Button share a further connection in that both are run by the Robertson family's management group, with Kimi being looked after by David's son Steve, a former rival of Mika Hakkinen in Formula Three before winning the 1994 Indy Lights title and racing in the British Touring Car Championship before turning to driver management.

THE NEXT HAKKINEN

Kimi won the Finnish and Nordic karting titles before he moved into car racing, testing a Formula Ford in Britain at the end of 1998. He was given his chance by Haywood Racing, the team that had just guided Button to the British Formula Ford title, and team boss Jim Warren was excited by the comparison. He said: "We did six tests with Button before he was really on the pace. Kimi was on it after the second." Encouraged by his speed, Haywood Racing promoted Kimi to its Mygale-chassised squad for the 1999

TRACK NOTES

Nationality . . . . FINNISH
Born . . . . OCTOBER 17, 1979,
ESPOO, FINLAND
Teams . . . . SAUBER 2001

CAREER RECORD

First Grand Prix 2001
AUSTRALIAN GP
Grand Prix starts 0
Grand Prix wins . . . . NONE
Pole . . . . NONE
Fastest laps . . . . NONE
Points . . . . NONE
Honours . . 2000 BRITISH FORMULA
RENAULT CHAMPION, 1999 BRITISH
FORMULA RENAULT WINTER SERIES
CHAMPION, 1998 EUROPEAN
SUPER A KART RUNNER-UP,
1998 FINNISH KART CHAMPION,
1998 NORDIC KART CHAMPION

British Formula Renault Championship. Third place on his debut against more experienced drivers reflected their faith, but after three more races his manager withdrew him from the series, upset at the superior performance of the Tatuus chassis run by Manor Motorsport, whose driver Antonio Pizzonia had been first to the finish in each of the first four races.

Kimi returned for the four-race Formula Renault winter series, this time driving for Manor Motorsport, and won all four of them from pole position with fastest lap to storm to the series title. Manor kept him on for a full British Formula Renault campaign in 2000. He won seven of the ten rounds he contested to clinch the title with two rounds to spare.

LOOKING AHEAD: Kimi has little racing past to consider, but a lot of future

ARROWS

ARROWS FIRE HIGH

Arrows made more progress than any other team during last year. For this year, they have replaced their Supertec engines with ex-works Peugeot engines badged as AMTs. Whether this is a step forward remains to be seen.

MIKE COUGHLAN

Rolls Royce may seem a world away from Formula One, but it was here that Mike trained as a student before hitting motor racing with Tiga Cars, gaining broad experience as he designed everything from Formula Fords to Group C sportscars. Mike started in Formula One with Lotus in 1984, then working at Benetton, Tyrrell and Ferrari before joining Arrows in 1997.

TOM WALKINSHAW

One of the leading characters in the pitlane. This former racer starred in touring cars, becoming European champion in 1984 before turning to team management. He guided Jaguar to victory at Le Mans in 1988, then turned to Formula One with Benetton in 1994. Tom ran Ligier before taking over Arrows in 1997. He also owns Gloucester Rugby Club.

THE MAJOR: Tom Walkinshaw controls all he sees in the Arrows camp, desperately aiming to lead Arrows to glory

Watch out for a change in the established order in 2001 as Arrows is changing its image. Seen by many as a team between Minardi and the back of the midfield, Arrows shifted up a gear last year and started to challenge for points on a regular basis. In the A21, it had an extremely sleek chassis, with its aerodynamic efficiency proved time and again in straightline speed tests. Give it a long straight and it was happy, as shown at Hockenheim, Spa-Francorchamps, Monza and Indianapolis. But this didn't always translate into a quick lap time as the car suffered in slow corners, and most circuits have those. Much of the credit for this must go to aerodynamicist Eghbal Hamidy, but before the season was out he was talking of heading off to Jordan. A tug of love then ensued and Hamidy was made to lay down the design of this year's A22 chassis before being allowed to move on, helping Arrows and hindering Jordan.

The Supertec engines, which were such a step up last year from the home-grown engines Arrows used in 1999, are being replaced with engines from the Asia Motor Technologies concern. In fact, these are last year's Peugeot engines rebadged, much as Renault engines became Mecachromes then Supertecs after the works deal was ended. Although they didn't shine with Prost last year, the AMT unit is shorter and lighter than the Supertec and said to be 10kg lighter, so it offers certain advantages, particularly in the sorting of the aerodynamic packaging. However, with the horsepower battle producing ever more power, the engineers at AMT's French base will have to work hard to keep Arrows in the fight.

Desiring continuity in this time of rebuilding the team, drivers Pedro de la Rosa and Jos Verstappen have been retained for 2001, offering the team welcome experience as it endeavours to continue its progress into the midfield and beyond.

FOR THE RECORD

Country of origin	England
Team base	Witney, England
Date of formation	1977
Active years in Formula One	From 1978
Grands Prix contested	354
Wins	NONE
Pole positions	NONE
Fastest laps	NONE

DRIVERS + RESULTS 2000

Driver	Nationality	Races	Wins	Pts	Pos
Pedro de la Rosa	Spanish	17	0	2	16th
Jos Verstappen	Dutch	17	0	5	12th

CAR SPECIFICATIONS

Sponsors	Orange, chello, Eurobet, Repsol
Team principal	Tom Walkinshaw
Team manager	tba
Technical director	Mike Coughlan
Chief engineer	tba
Test driver	tba
Chassis	Arrows A22
Engine	AMT Peugeot V10
Tyres	Bridgestone

CALLING MAJOR TOM: Mike Coughlan reports to Tom Walkinshaw on all the team's technical matters

SIGNS OF PROMISE

De la Rosa was joined by Verstappen in an eleventh-hour deal last year. Yet, if Verstappen's signing was last minute, it was nothing compared with that of sponsor Orange, with the livery literally drying as the cars went out for the first practice session at Melbourne. Using Supertec engines for the first time, Arrows clawed back some of the horsepower deficit it had endured in 1998 when running its own engines. There were no points at the opening race this time. Indeed, Arrows had to wait until the sixth round at the Nurburgring for de la Rosa to get into the points, in sixth. Verstappen then went one better by finishing fifth in Montreal. But the clearest sign that the team was making progress came at the A1-Ring when de la Rosa avoided the carnage at the first corner and was running comfortably in third until his gearbox failed. He showed well again next time out, at Hockenheim, qualifying fifth and finishing sixth. But then his year

was nearly brought to an end at Monza when he was sent cartwheeling in the first-lap accident, coming to rest upside down on top of Rubens Barrichello's Ferrari. Fortunately he was uninjured, and Verstappen put a smile back on their faces by racing strongly to fourth.

SO NEAR, AND YET SO FAR

Arrows was formed in 1978 by a group of the leading personnel from Shadow, including Jackie Oliver, Alan Rees and designer Tony Southgate. Despite Riccardo Patrese retiring from the lead on the team's second appearance, at Kyalami, an Arrows didn't lead a race again until the 1997 Hungarian Grand Prix when Damon Hill led until halfway around the final lap, and that elusive first win is still being awaited after 354 Grands Prix.

Patrese was the backbone of the team until 1981, with Marc Surer, Thierry Boutsen, Derek Warwick, Eddie Cheever and Michele Alboreto all staying for several years, but none ever winning. The Japanese Footwork corporation took over the team in 1990, but after four years it departed and Oliver and Rees were back in charge. Then, in 1996, Tom Walkinshaw bought control and has fought to gain the backing to take the team forward, with the signing of sponsor Orange last year constituting a major coup.

JOS VERSTAPPEN

DOUBLE DUTCH

New engines from AMT ought to help Dutchman Jos Verstappen and Arrows to continue the progress that they displayed through 2000. Once one of the young guns himself, the Dutchman is actually one of the old school now.

Jos Verstappen has spent his career flitting in and out of Formula One, so he will be delighted to be enjoying a second straight season with Arrows in 2001. His contract negotiations with Arrows were drawn out but, for once, Jos knew for whom he would be driving with months in hand before the start of the season. Indeed, his main concern while pen was being put to contract was over a court case in which he

DESPERATE FOR SUCCESS: Jos needs results this year if he is to remain in Formula One

was found guilty of assault. An out-of-court settlement has left Jos clear to focus on 2001 when his and team-mate Pedro de la Rosa's progress will be determined by the performance of the ex-works Peugeot engines that are now badged as AMTs.

Jos's other concern will be that he matches the pace of de la Rosa, for although he scored five points to the Spaniard's two last year, he was outqualified by the Spaniard 12 times to five. His points came from fifth in the Canadian Grand Prix, then fourth at Monza in a race that was shorn of five of its top eight drivers.

FAST ROUTE TO THE TOP

Jos was a karting champion in Holland and Belgium, but his progress once he stepped up to cars was stunning as he won the Benelux Formula Opel title at his first attempt in 1992. He then won the 1993 German Formula Three title. A Formula One test at Estoril stunned onlookers as Jos lapped a Footwork only fractionally slower than regular driver Derek Warwick had qualified for the Portuguese Grand Prix. Signed as test driver by Benetton, Jos contested the first two Grands Prix of 1994 after JJ Lehto broke his neck, just two years after his first car race.

Jos's debut was marked by a massive shunt at Interlagos. Then, later that year, Jos was lucky to survive a pitlane fire in the German Grand Prix. He bounced back to finish third at the Hungaroring and Spa-Francorchamps, but was dropped by Benetton for 1995. Strong showings for Simtek were scuppered when the team folded, leaving him without a drive.

Thin years with Arrows in 1996 and Tyrrell

in 1997 followed. As scoring points has never been easy with a tail-end team, this left Jos on the sidelines, but he bounced back midway through 1998 when he took over from Jan Magnussen in the second Stewart seat. When no points followed, Jos dropped from Formula One for a second time and didn't return until 2000.

PEDRO DE LA ROSA

IN THE ASCENDANCY

Pedro de la Rosa was one of the stars of 2000. After all, anyone who manages to run in third place in an Arrows must be doing something right, and he did it several times. If Arrows continues to progress, then so will Pedro.

LOOKING FOR POINTS: Pedro ran well on occasion last year and is very eager to score more points in 2001

TRACK NOTES

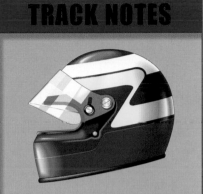

Nationality	SPANISH
Born	FEBRUARY 24, 1971, BARCELONA, SPAIN
Teams	ARROWS 1999-2001

CAREER RECORD

First Grand Prix	1999 AUSTRALIAN GP
Grand Prix starts	33
Grand Prix wins	NONE
	(best result: sixth in 1999 Australian GP, 2000 European GP, 2000 German GP)
Poles	NONE
Fastest laps	NONE
Points	3
Honours	1997 FORMULA NIPPON CHAMPION, 1995 JAPANESE FORMULA THREE CHAMPION, 1992 EUROPEAN & BRITISH FORMULA RENAULT CHAMPION, 1990 SPANISH FORMULA FORD CHAMPION

Spanish driver Pedro de la Rosa has a reputation for being cool, intelligent and efficient. Last year, he added 'quick' to his list of attributes, so a strong run with Arrows this year could open the door for a move to a team nearer the front of the grid.

Qualifying in the middle of the grid for the opening race last year showed that Arrows had made progress over its 1999 position. Suspension failure brought that meeting to a halt for him, but that was nothing next to the disappointment he endured on his home track at Barcelona when he qualified ninth, only to be consigned to the back of the grid because of a fuel irregularity.

Sixth place at the Nurburgring yielded the first point of his campaign, but he'd run third in the mixed conditions. Germany seemed to suit Pedro, as he next scored when the circus visited Hockenheim, again finishing sixth after running fourth by making the most of the car's straightline speed. This performance came one race after Pedro had run incredibly strongly at the A1-Ring, looking comfortable in third before he retired with gearbox failure.

The moment for which most people will remember Pedro in 2000 is the scary accident at Monza when he was involved in the pile-up at the second chicane and went airborne after hitting Johnny Herbert's Jaguar, climbing 20ft into the air before rolling to a halt in the gravel trap.

A LONG, HARD PASSAGE

Pedro worked long and hard to make it to Formula One, with a career that appeared on occasion to have stalled. The national Formula Ford champion in his native Spain in 1990, Pedro picked up backing from his national sporting federation and headed to contest the more competitive British championships. After winning the British and European Formula Renault titles in 1992, Pedro moved up to British Formula Three, but his hopes of going for gold in 1994 were scuppered by a wrong choice of engine. With this lack of results limiting his budget, he headed for a paid ride in Japanese Formula Three in 1995, and he won every round but one, when he finished second. Pedro progressed to Formula Nippon – Japan's version of Formula 3000 – winning the title in 1997. He then became a test driver for Jordan in 1998, before his Repsol backing landed him his Formula One break with Arrows in 1999, where he got in the points on his debut by finishing sixth.

JAGUAR RACING

SECOND TIME LUCKY?

Jaguar promised the earth and promptly fell flat on its face in its debut season last year. Points were as rare as hen's teeth, and a major shake-up has been undertaken over the winter to ensure progress is made in 2001.

THE VIPS

BOBBY RAHAL

A three-time ChampCar champion – in 1986, 1987 and 1992 – Bobby raced first in Formula Three and then Formula Two, also having two Grand Prix outings with Wolf in 1978. He retired to run his own ChampCar team, then briefly took the helm of ChampCar's organizing body last year before jumping at this opening.

STEVE NICHOLS

The team's newly-signed chief designer has an illustrious history that includes the entire 1980s at McLaren – the team's greatest years. He worked at Ferrari from 1990 to 1992, then Sauber and Jordan and McLaren again, running future projects.

THE CHAIRMAN: Neil Ressler has confronted the team's failings in its first year and made changes

B obby Rahal – a driver who contested just two Grands Prix before heading home to the USA for glory in the ChampCar series – could be the key ingredient in making Jaguar take a step forward after a disappointing maiden season in Formula One.

One of Rahal's first signings as he and Jaguar chairman Neil Ressler – the man who headed up Jaguar Racing in 2000 – tried to bolster the team's personnel was aerodynamicist Mark Handford. They had talked of trying to lure Formula One's top aerodynamicist Adrian Newey away from McLaren, but failed. Rahal knows Handford well from his work in ChampCars with Lola, and Handford knows Formula One well,

having worked for Team Haas, Tyrrell and Benetton. Eddie Irvine has been retained as the team's number-one driver, with Brazilian driver Luciano Burti being promoted from Jaguar's test team.

A TROUBLED FIRST YEAR

Calling Jaguar's 2000 campaign its first is misleading, as the main new ingredients were the team name and a new green livery sprayed over the top of the infrastructure of the three-year-old Stewart that it bought out and took over. Most of the personnel were carried, the design team was much the same, and so was the engine supplier. Johnny Herbert – scorer of Stewart's only

win – was kept on in the driving force, joined by Ferrari's 1999 world title challenger Irvine. But the package simply didn't gel.

At the start of the year, Irvine was qualifying relatively well. He was running in a comfortable sixth position in the Brazilian Grand Prix before he pressed too hard and went off. Had he known how hard points were to be to come by, he would probably have shown a little more caution. Indeed, he was to score only twice all year. One of the team's major problems was the fact that its cars simply wouldn't get off the line cleanly, both drivers regularly losing two or three places at the start. The rear end was wayward too, and it was this that caught Irvine out at Interlagos.

FOR THE RECORD

Country of origin	England
Team base	Milton Keynes, England
Date of formation	1987 (as Paul Stewart Racing)
Active years in Formula One	From 1997 (as Stewart)
Grands Prix contested	66
Wins	1
Pole positions	1
Fastest laps	NONE

DRIVERS + RESULTS 2000

Driver	Nationality	Races	Wins	Pts	Pos
Eddie Irvine	Northern Irish	17	0	4	13th
Johnny Herbert	English	17	0	0	N/A

CAR SPECIFICATIONS

Sponsors	Jaguar, HSBC, Becks, DHL, WorldCom, Hewlett-Packard
Chairman	Neil Ressler
Chief Executive Officer	Bobby Rahal
Designer	Steve Nichols
Chief engineer	Alex Varnava
Test driver	Tomas Scheckter
Chassis	Jaguar R2
Engine	Jaguar V10
Tyres	Michelin

Add to that the fact that the engine wasn't operating to its potential and that the aerodynamics needed attention, and it's not so surprising that Jaguar wasn't up there leading the battle to be the best of the rest behind the Ferraris and McLarens.

Irvine recorded Jaguar's best result with fourth place at Monaco, while Herbert never finished higher than seventh – at the A1-Ring and Suzuka – and knew that he was out of a drive before the summer was over. There were clear signs in the closing races that progress was being made, with their seventh and eighth places at Suzuka looking solid in a race of few retirements. But they were still a lap away from winning, so there's room for improvement.

THE DAYS OF STEWART

To analyse Jaguar's previous form, one has to look to the three seasons of Formula One that Stewart Grand Prix completed before the takeover. Formed from Paul Stewart Racing that had run teams in Formula 3000 and Formula Three, with healthy backing from Ford and with three-time World Champion Jackie Stewart at the helm, the team employed Rubens Barrichello and Jan Magnussen. Its first year, 1997, was marked by a surprise second place for Barrichello at Monaco and by numerous engine failures. Disappointing form led to Magnussen being replaced by Jos Verstappen midway through a less-impressive 1998 season. Then Herbert filled the number-two seat in 1999, and read changing weather conditions best to give the team its one-and-only win at the Nurburgring, elevating the team to its best-ever position in the Constructors' Cup: fourth.

CAT AT A STANDSTILL: Johnny Herbert waits patiently during a pitstop in last year's Brazilian Grand Prix

EDDIE IRVINE

JAGUAR'S TOP CAT

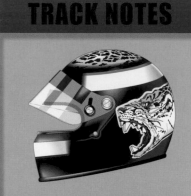

Life as a number-one driver wasn't as wonderful last year as Eddie Irvine had hoped. He knew that leaving Ferrari for Jaguar Racing was a gamble, but it's just that it looks to be more of a long-term investment than a quick profit.

Nationality	. . . . . NORTHERN IRISH
Born	. . . . NOVEMBER 10, 1965,
	CONLIG, NORTHERN IRELAND
Teams	. . . . . . JORDAN 1993–1995,
	FERRARI 1996–1999,
	JAGUAR RACING 2000–2001

CAREER RECORD

First Grand Prix	 1993
	JAPANESE GP
Grand Prix starts	 113
Grand Prix wins	 4
	1999 Australian GP,
1999 Austrian GP,	1999 German GP,
	1999 Malaysian GP
Poles	. . . . NONE
Fastest laps	 1
Points	 177
Honours	. . . . 1993 JAPANESE
	FORMULA 3000 RUNNER-UP,
	1987 BRITISH FORMULA FORD
	CHAMPION & FORMULA FORD
	FESTIVAL WINNER

FOND MEMORIES: Eddie must have looked back wistfully to his Ferrari days during 2000

A fter four years at Ferrari, Eddie Irvine's life was turned upside down last year. He swapped a red car for a green one. He went from being number two to Michael Schumacher to being the team leader in his new camp. And he stopped winning races. All of this was expected. What he hadn't contemplated was that he would almost stop scoring points, managing to do so just twice in 17 Grands Prix.

Embroiled in a title battle with McLaren's Mika Hakkinen until the final round in 1999, Eddie was brought back to earth with a bump. While the top teams progressed, the Stewart team's transformation to Jaguar led to a decline in its relative form. Finishing races was a problem, and although Eddie's spin into retirement from sixth in the Brazilian Grand Prix was a mistake, he made amends by finishing fourth at Monaco. This proved to be his best result of the year, with sixth in the final round at Sepang his only other score, and he did not win the

affection of everyone in the team as the problems mounted. His insouciant manner convinced some that he wasn't trying. However, team boss Neil Ressler could see that he was giving 100%, and his qualifying positions in the first half of the year – sixth at Interlagos and at Magny-Cours – showed that he could string together a fast lap when the car was up to it.

A LONG APPRENTICESHIP

Eddie was racing before Jenson Button was old enough to race a kart. British Formula Ford Champion in 1987, he was fifth in British Formula Three then third overall in Formula 3000 for Eddie Jordan Racing in 1990. This failed to open the door to a Formula One ride, so Eddie headed to Japan,

to be paid extremely well to race in their Formula 3000 series.

He was given his Formula One break by Jordan at the end of 1993, when he not only raced to sixth at Suzuka, but earned the wrath of Ayrton Senna for repassing him after being lapped. Two years with Jordan produced a best result of third in Montreal in 1995, so it was a surprise when he was signed by Ferrari for 1996. Suffering by having to play the support role to Schumacher, he scored his first win at Melbourne in 1999, and was then elevated to number-one status when Schumacher broke his leg. Wins then followed, first of all at the A1-Ring, and then at Hockenheim and Sepang, but he was ultimately beaten to the title by Mika Hakkinen.

LUCIANO BURTI

Luciano Burti was given a taster of Formula One racing last year when he subbed for Eddie Irvine in Austria, but Jaguar's test driver has moved up to a full-time racing seat for 2001.

TRACK NOTES

Nationality	BRAZILIAN
Born	MAY 3, 1975, BRAZIL
Teams	JAGUAR RACING 2001

CAREER RECORD

First Grand Prix	2000
	AUSTRIAN GP
Grand Prix starts	1
Grand Prix wins	NONE
(best result: 11th, 2000 Austrian GP)	
Poles	NONE
Fastest laps	NONE
Points	0
Honours	1999 BRITISH
FORMULA THREE RUNNER-UP,	
1997 BRITISH FORMULA	
VAUXHALL CHAMPION	

Jaguar rather than race in Formula 3000. This was at the behest of mentor Jackie Stewart for whom he raced in Formula Three, the three-time World Champion believing that there's no better preparation for a career in the sport's top category. Stewart's advice was correct, for his testing stint not only landed Luciano Jaguar's second race seat for 2001, but it gave him a one-off race opportunity when Eddie Irvine wasn't well enough to race in last year's Austrian Grand Prix. A solid eleventh-place finish gave Luciano useful race mileage.

The big question is how Luciano will stack up against Irvine. Popular within the team he may be, but Irvine is the man with the experience as well as being the contracted number one, so Luciano will be expected to get his head down and learn his racing craft, hoping that Jaguar will offer him a more competitive package than they offered last year. If he is able to show half as much form as Button did last year for Williams, then Luciano will have done well. Don't discount it, though, as he comes recommended for his intellectual approach, so ought to be able to squeeze a lot from the car.

TEAMS UP WITH STEWART

Luciano started in karts, like all his contemporaries, graduating to Formula Ford. However, he left his native Brazil to come to Britain in 1996, after convincing his father he was mature enough to make a career in racing. Racing in the Vauxhall Junior Championship, he finished as runner-up in a team run by former Formula One racer Martin Donnelly. Driving for Paul Stewart Racing in 1997, Luciano won the British Formula Vauxhall Championship. He advanced to

MOVING UP A STEP: Being test driver yielded one race last year, but the big prize was the team's number two seat for the 2001 Championship

British Formula Three in 1998, staying on with PSR. He won twice and ended the year third overall behind compatriots Mario Haberfeld and Enrique Bernoldi. Staying on with PSR for 1999, he won five times but was beaten to the title by Marc Hynes. He did, however, outscore Button to end the year as runner-up.

The 25-year-old Brazilian is a classic case of a driver taking the twenty-first century approach to landing a top ride in Formula One: via the team's test outfit. An arch-rival of Jenson Button in British Formula Three in 1999, Burti opted to test for

MINARDI

HANGING ON IN THERE

Armed with its biggest-ever budget, Minardi will be trying to fight its way off the back of the grid. But, the withdrawal of engine supplier Mugen has left Minardi to fight its way with slightly long-in-the-tooth Supertec engines in 2001.

THE VIPS

GIANCARLO MINARDI

The departure of long-time partner Gabriele Rumi last year means that Giancarlo is again the team's figurehead. This 53-year-old Fiat dealer ran a race-winning team in Formula Two before stepping up to Formula One. He has worked miracles to stay in the World Championship since then.

GUSTAV BRUNNER

Gustav brought more than 20 years of Formula One design experience with him when he joined Minardi from Ferrari in 1998. The Austrian had worked previously for ATS, Ferrari for the first time, Rial, Zakspeed, Leyton House and Minardi for the first time. After his travels, he enjoys the family atmosphere at Minardi.

GOOD NEWS AND BAD NEWS: Giancarlo Minardi was excited by news that Minardi had found financial salvation, then it fell through

Talk of Minardi being sold to its Spanish sponsor Telefonica and a move to Spain for its base ran throughout the spring and summer of 2000, but they came to nought. The team would remain in Italy, but it would also remain short of cash. Then in stepped a new source of the finance needed to develop the team. This came when long-time team partner and principal shareholder Gabriele Rumi sold his two-thirds share of the team last September to PSN, the Argentinian Pan American Sports Network International, ending a 15-year involvement in Formula One since his Fondmetal company started supplying lightweight wheels to several teams. He subsequently entered his own team, Fondmetal, from 1990 to 1992 before buying a stake in Minardi in 1996 and putting the team on a sounder financial footing than ever before. However, Rumi decided that PSN's larger budget would help the team more and stood aside. But then PSN withdrew and this threw the team into turmoil. At the time of writing, just after Christmas, Gaston Mazzacane is tipped to stay for a second season, most likely being joined by Spaniard Fernando Alonso, one of the brightest lights in last year's Formula 3000 series.

It had been assumed until last November that Minardi's M03s would be powered by Mugen Honda engines, as used by Jordan in 2000, but the Japanese company withdrew, leaving Minardi with the limited choice of Supertec. Although Supertecs weren't the weakest engines on the grid in 2000, the ex-Renault engines aren't expected to be developed now that Renault is returning with works engines for Benetton.

PROGRESS MADE

Minardi were traditionally on the back row of the grid, as before, but their gap to the teams ahead had come down, suggesting that the team was making real progress. Much of this must go down to a budget from sponsor Telefonica that offered the team development money that had been absent before. Certainly, designer Gustav Brunner had

A FAMILY ENVIRONMENT: Gaston Mazzacane appreciated the Italian team's close-knit atmosphere as he found his feet in Formula One

produced a very tidy chassis. Had it been mated to an engine more powerful than the Ford customer engine they used, the car might have been closer to joining those from the midfield teams. On top of that, in drivers Gene and Argentinian rookie Mazzacane, it didn't have the quickest drivers in Formula One. Gene finished in eighth place in the opening race, suggesting that its 1999 tally of one point would be matched in at least one of the races, but as only nine cars finished, perhaps not. Mazzacane matched this finish in the European Grand Prix before Gene was eighth for a second time at the A1-Ring. But that was to be as close as they got, as their travel money for 2001 went up in smoke.

THE OTHER ITALIAN TEAM

Minardi progressed from Formula Two to Formula One in 1985, and here it has stayed ever since, albeit almost invariably at the tail of the field, scoring just 28 points since then. Pierluigi Martini was the team's standard bearer in that first year, then Alessandro Nannini was the number one for the next two years as the team struggled with Motori Moderni engines before Martini returned in 1988 and used Ford power to score the team's first point. Their fortune improved six-fold in 1989, with Martini bagging a couple of fifth places and briefly leading at Estoril. However, it was in 1990 that the team had its greatest moment, when Martini qualified on the front row for the season-opener at Phoenix, thanks to making the most of super qualifying tyres from Pirelli. Yet not a point was scored all year. Using ex-works Ferrari engines in 1991, Martini claimed a pair of fourth-place finishes as Minardi ranked seventh. And this was to be the high point of the team's history, with Christian Fittipaldi's fourth place at Kyalami in 1993 the only other good result since then. This run of failure looked to be coming to an end in 1999 when Luca Badoer was heading for fourth at the Nurburgring, until his car stuttered to a halt.

Minardi may not have a reputation for scoring lots of points, but it does have one for introducing young talent to Formula One, including Giancarlo Fisichella and Jarno Trulli.

FOR THE RECORD

Country of origin	Italy
Team base	Faenza, Italy
Date of formation	1980
Active years in Formula One	From 1985
Grands Prix contested	254
Wins	NONE
Pole positions	NONE
Fastest laps	NONE

DRIVERS + RESULTS 2000

Driver	Nationality	Races	Wins	Pts	Pos
Marc Gene	Spanish	17	0	0	N/A
Gaston Mazzacane	Argentinian	17	0	0	N/A

CAR SPECIFICATIONS

Sponsors	Leaseplan, DOIMO, Cocif
Team principal	Giancarlo Minardi
Team manager	Frederic Dhainaut
Designer	Gustav Brunner
Chief engineer	Gabriele Tredozi
Test driver	tba
Chassis	Minardi M03
Engine	Mecachrome V10
Tyres	tba

GASTON MAZZACANE*

A SPONSOR'S FAVOURITE

Being the sponsor's choice has helped Gaston Mazzacane to remain in Formula One for a second season after only really managing to reach the end of last year's Grands Prix rather than drive fast in his first year with Minardi.

SURPRISE PACKAGE: Not many expected Gaston to become a Formula One driver, but this he did in 2000

Minardi lost its lead sponsor Telefonica at the end of last season. The Spanish telecommunications giant had wanted Spanish-speaking drivers, but it was still thought that Argentinian Gaston Mazzacane would be shown the door. After all, he hadn't set any speed records in his maiden season of Formula One. But his skin appeared to be saved when the majority of the shares in the team were bought by Argentinian television conglomerate Pan-American Sports Network. But then the deal

fell through. At the time of writing, he had yet to decide whether to stay on or follow PSN to fill the second seat at Prost.

Analysing the statistics of Gaston's maiden season shows that he came out second best to team-mate Marc Gene. Neither scored any points, but the little-rated Spaniard was often a second faster in qualifying, and Gaston's shining virtue was that he was usually still circulating at the end. His best result from his 12 finishes in the 17 Grands Prix was eighth at the Nurburgring when he was still two laps adrift.

FROM KARTS TO SPORTSCARS

After three years of racing karts, Gaston raced in Argentina's Datsun 280ZX Cup in 1992, as he wasn't old enough to race in Argentina's single-seater series. Having ranked fourth overall, he then leapt into Formula Three in 1993, finishing second in the junior class of the South American series. Instead of staying for a second year and gunning for race wins and outright championship honours, Gaston headed for Italy. There he contested and won the Italian Formula 2000 series – a club racing category for year-old Formula Three cars. Racing in the Italian Formula Three Championship in 1995, Gaston was only 11th overall. However, not wanting to hang around, he moved up to Formula 3000 in 1996 and stayed there until 1998 when he twice scored points with a pair of sixth places. This tally didn't seem the result of having driven for a tail-end team – his team-mate won races in 1997 and 1998.

However, Gaston's first win since 1994 came in 1999 after he'd turned his back on

single-seaters and was racing in the SportsRacing World Cup, when he shared a Ferrari with Giovanni Lavaggi – another driver who had bought himself a ride at Minardi – and won at Magny-Cours. Despite taking the Minardi test ride, few thought he had series Formula One ambitions...

TRACK NOTES

Nationality . . . . ARGENTINIAN
Born . . . . MAY 8, 1975,
BUENOS AIRES, ARGENTINA
Teams . . . . . . MINARDI 2000-2001

CAREER RECORD

First Grand Prix 2000
AUSTRALIAN GP
Grand Prix starts 17
Grand Prix wins . . . . NONE
(best result: eighth in 2000 European GP)
Poles . . . . NONE
Fastest laps . . . . NONE
Points . . . . NONE
Honours . . . . 1994 ITALIAN
FORMULA 2000 CHAMPION

*This driver for this team was provisional at the time of going to press and had not been confirmed

FERNANDO ALONSO*

SPAIN'S GREAT WHITE HOPE

Fernando Alonso is a driver about whom everyone is excited. He attracted Ferrari's interest, so getting Flavio Briatore's attention, who put him on a contract in return for Supertec engines for Minardi and a ride for Fernando.

Twelve months ago, only the sport's cognoscenti knew of Fernando Alonso. In twelve months time, as with Jenson Button last year, you can be sure that people throughout racing will be unable to recall that he'd never been famous. The Spanish 19-year-old won't have made his name for being at the front of the midfield, challenging, as Jenson was, since he will be driving for Minardi not Williams, but his skills are such that Spanish fans in particular will have plenty to shout about.

Hovering on the wings of Formula One, looking likely to collect a test ride, Fernando was propelled into the frame at the start of last December when Benetton offered him a run in one of its cars. This just served to emphasise quite how keen the Benetton team chief Flavio Briatore was to stop Ferrari from snapping up Fernando Alonso's services.

At the time of writing, It's presumed that he has signed a long-term contract with Benetton, but will be loaned to Minardi as part of the team's deal to run Supertec engines.

It's currently the fashion to look to drivers in the nursery formulae and pluck them straight to Formula One on either a testing contract or even a race contract. However, despite Fernando's youth, he already has two seasons of experience in powerful slicks and wings formulae, and this will be a huge help when it comes to the actual racing in Formula One.

RAPID PROGRESS

After a brief and extremely successful karting career, Fernando advanced into car racing, taking the huge step straight into the Spanish-based Open Fortuna Championship – for cars not far short of Formula 3000 performance – in 1999.

Racing for a team run by former Minardi driver Adrian Campos, Fernando showed outstanding talent to win six rounds and pip Portuguese rival Manuel Giao to the title. Not only did this impress onlookers, but so did his form in 2000 when he tested for Minardi, which was part of his prize for winning the title.

Moving up to Formula 3000 in 2000, Fernando set outstanding testing times straight away and was immediately seen as a dark horse, someone to challenge the favoured drivers of experience. He didn't disappoint as he finished the year ranked fourth overall thanks to finishing second and then first in the final two rounds for Astromega, giving the Belgian team a huge boost on its home circuit. The speed had been evident all season and it had finally borne fruit.

A NEW FACE: Fernando Alonso offers Spain a new star to cheer

TRACK NOTES

Nationality	SPANISH
Born	JULY 29, 1981, SPAIN
Teams	MINARDI 2001?

CAREER RECORD

First Grand Prix	2001 AUSTRALIAN GP
Grand Prix starts	NONE
Grand Prix wins	NONE
Poles	NONE
Fastest laps	NONE
Points	NONE
Honours	1999 FORMULA OPEN FORTUNA WITH NISSAN CHAMPION, 1997 ITALIAN & SPANISH KART CHAMPION, 1996 WORLD & JUNIOR KART CHAMPION, 1993-1996 SPANISH JUNIOR KART CHAMPION

*This driver for this team was provisional at the time of going to press and had not been confirmed

PROST

LOOKING FOR SALVATION

Prost ended last year bottom of the 11 teams, and lost both its longtime sponsor and its engine supplier. So, the only way is up in 2001, with pluses coming from a deal to run Ferrari engines and the boost to its finances by the arrival of Pedro Diniz in a management role.

Few teams had to endure as much wheeler-dealing as Prost did last year. Not only did team boss Alain Prost have to go looking for a new engine supplier following a falling-out with Peugeot, but he had to find a new sponsor as the team suffered a huge blow last September when the Altadis Group, parent company of Gauloises, withdrew its sponsorship. Not only did this bring to an end a partnership that had lasted from 1976, but it left the team £12 million short in its budget.

Then, with no works engine deals in the offing, Prost did a two-year deal to run ex-Ferrari engines. Strong engines they may be, but they will have to be paid for, with a budget of £16 million thought necessary to cover the bill. As with the deal enjoyed by Sauber since 1997, these engines will always be one year of specification behind the works engines.

A beacon of continuity in a sea of change is the fact that Jean Alesi will be staying on for a second season, with Pedro Diniz joining

THE VIPS

PEDRO DINIZ

Pedro raced karts and then Formula Three in Brazil before trying British Formula Three in 1991. Advancing to Formula 3000 in 1993 didn't produce blinding results, with one fourth place in 1994 his best result, but he graduated to Formula One with Forti in 1995. Wanting a competitive car, he joined Ligier in 1996. Spells at Arrows and Sauber followed before Pedro decided to turn to management.

ALAIN PROST

He has had a torrid time as a team owner, but people should never forget that Alain was four times the Formula One World Champion. European Formula Three champion in 1979, he leapt straight to Formula One, winning 51 Grands Prix in all – a record total that only Michael Schumacher looks likely to challenge – for Renault, McLaren and Williams before turning to team management in 1996.

UNUSUAL SHOT: The Prost cars were seldom a blur of glorious colour and success last year

FOR THE RECORD

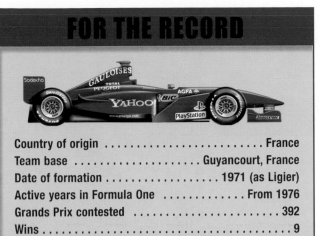

Country of origin . . . . France
Team base . . . . Guyancourt, France
Date of formation . . . . 1971 (as Ligier)
Active years in Formula One . . . . From 1976
Grands Prix contested 392
Wins 9
Pole positions 9
Fastest laps 11

DRIVERS + RESULTS 2000

Driver	Nationality	Races	Wins	Pts	Pos
Jean Alesi	French	17	0	0	N/A
Nick Heidfeld	German	17	0	0	N/A

CAR SPECIFICATIONS

Sponsors . . . . PSN, Playstation
Team principal . . . . Alain Prost
Managing director . . . . Joan Villadelprat
Technical director . . . . Henri Durand
Designer . . . . Jean-Paul Gousset
Chief engineer . . . . Vincent Gaillardot
Test driver . . . . tba
Chassis . . . . Prost AP04
Engine . . . . Ferrari V10
Tyres . . . . Michelin

the team from Sauber and bringing with him backing that should prove a lifeline to the team. The Brazilian should also recognize a few of the faces, having driven for the team when it was still called Ligier back in 1996. At the time of writing, the team's second driver has not been announced, but the signing of PSN as team sponsor suggests that pre-Christmas favourite Enrique Bernoldi may be replaced by Gaston Mazzacane, perhaps in a straight swap with Minardi.

Poor management is a charge that has been levelled at the team, and steps have been taken in this area. As a result, Joan Villadelprat is the new managing director, bringing with him experience of working at Ferrari, McLaren and most recently Benetton. He will relieve the pressure on Alain Prost by taking responsibility for the day-to-day running of the team, leaving Prost to concentrate on global strategy and overall supervision. On top of this, aerodynamicist Henri Durand has come on board from McLaren.

A POINTLESS YEAR

Prost's 2000 World Championship campaign is one that the team will wish to forget. Frequent tussles with engine supplier Peugeot, endless talks of a team take-over and not a point on the board after 17 Grands Prix, even with that inveterate point-scorer Alesi giving his all. Examine the French ace's record of just five finishes and it's easy to see why. There were moments of promise, such as when he made the right tyre choice and rocketed from 17th to fourth as the track dried in the Belgian Grand Prix. Then the car broke. Team-mate Nick Heidfeld was also hit hard by retirements, peaking with eighth place.

A TALE OF TWO TEAMS

To understand the history of Prost fully, one must include the history of the Ligier team from which it evolved after Alain Prost took the team over in 1997. This takes us all the way back to 1976 when the all-French team burst onto the Formula One scene with its extraordinarily-shaped JS5, known as the "Tea Pot". Jacques Laffite pedalled this to second place in Austria. Impressively, the team went one better in 1977 when he won in Sweden. Matra engines were swapped for a Ford DFV in 1979 and the team promptly dominated the start of the season, Laffite winning twice and team mate Patrick Depailler once in the first five races. Their advantage was negated, though, and they slipped to third overall. This was improved on in 1980 when Ligier ranked second only to Williams, with Laffite and Didier Pironi winning one apiece. That, though, was the high point of Ligier – even though Laffite won twice in 1981 – and the team's next win was courtesy of Olivier Panis 15 years later in the wet at Monaco. Since Prost took over, though, the team has slumped, with only the 1997 season offering anything to cheer about, when Panis was third in Brazil and second in Spain before breaking his legs in Canada, and replacement Jarno Trulli led the Austrian Grand Prix. Second place in the Nurburgring scramble of 1999 lifted a season that otherwise offered little.

DESPERATELY SEEKING SUCCESS: Alain Prost had a stormy ride through 2000 and is looking for better form

JEAN ALESI

JEAN'S LAST CHANCE SALOON

Now one of the ten most experienced Grand Prix drivers of all time, Jean Alesi is returning for a thirteenth season in Formula One. However, by continuing with Prost, he's unlikely to add to his only Grand Prix win, scored back in 1995.

TRACK NOTES

Nationality . . . . FRENCH
Born . . . . JUNE 11, 1964,
AVIGNON, FRANCE
Teams . . . . . . TYRRELL 1989-1990
FERRARI 1991-1995
BENETTON 1996-1997
SAUBER 1998-1999
PROST 2000-2001

CAREER RECORD

First Grand Prix 1989
FRENCH GP
Grand Prix starts 184
Grand Prix wins 1
(1995 Canadian GP)
Poles 2
Fastest laps 4
Points 236
Honours . . . . 1989 FORMULA
3000 CHAMPION, 1987 FRENCH
FORMULA THREE CHAMPION

A SIGN OF THINGS TO COME: Jean Alesi retired from last year's opening race and his season failed to improve

Jean Alesi begins 2001 with 184 Grand Prix starts to his name, but his one win is way short of the tally you'd expect of a driver of his calibre. Looking at the year ahead, you can be sure that unless something incredible occurs he won't be scoring win number two in a Prost.

King of mixed conditions when he uses his skills on a wet/dry track, Jean doesn't want to leave Formula One and he's faithful to good friend Alain Prost, but there were times last year when you wondered why. Indeed, Jean suggested that the car's aerodynamic problems were so bad that he might have done a better job on the bridge in his home town with a ball of wool than the aerodynamicists did in the windtunnel...

Poor Jean really suffered during his first campaign with Prost. Unfortunately the car never really looked like scoring points and was seldom around at the finish. However, there were moments when his ability shone through, such as at the Belgian Grand Prix when he came in early for dry tyres and shot from seventeenth to fourth. Then his engine failed him, and so his best result was ninth at the Nurburgring.

A DOUBLE CHAMPION

Jean started racing cars before Jenson Button had even started school. That was in 1983 when he made his debut in the French Renault 5 series. Turning to single-seaters in 1984, Jean raced in Formula Renault for two years, and was then runner-up in French Formula Three in 1986. Champion the following year, he moved up to Formula 3000 in 1988. However, it was in 1989 that he won that championship with Eddie Jordan Racing. Midway through that year he made his Formula One debut for Tyrrell, replacing Michele Alboreto. Fourth on his debut, he improved on this in 1990 when he raced to second in the opening race at Phoenix after a great tussle with Ayrton Senna. This was backed up with a second at Monaco. Ferrari signed him for 1991. He finally scored his first win at Montreal in 1995, then moved to Benetton. Two years there yielded no more wins, but a lot of points as Jean proved himself to be one of the most consistent finishers, managing fourth overall in 1996 and 1997. Two years followed at Sauber without much in the way of results before he moved on to Prost.

ENRIQUE BERNOLDI*

F1

BRAZILIAN BRAVADO

Enrique Bernoldi wanted to step up from test seat to race seat. But Kimi Raikkonen stole his opening. Instead of a third season in Formula 3000, Enrique clinched a race seat with Prost.

Talk to Enrique Bernoldi, and he is one of those drivers who gives the impression that he will be quick. Everything about his darty demeanour suggests this, but he hasn't produced the results to match this yet, with Enrique's mental toughness being questioned. However, for all that and the disappointment of losing out on the second Sauber seat, he recovered to be in a position when we closed for press to land the second seat at Prost. Not afraid of racing abroad – he's raced for Italian, British and Austrian teams – his stay at this French team will be aided by Brazilian racer-turned-team boss Diniz if he manages to land the drive ahead of Gaston Mazzacane.

A EUROPEAN EDUCATION

Enrique was one of the stars of Brazil's karting circles, winning the Sao Paulo state's junior karting championship before landing the national junior title in 1990 and 1991. Widening his aim as he got older, Enrique took in the South American and PanAmerican championships in 1993, being ranked third and fourth respectively. Next he packed his bags for Europe in 1995, aged 16. His first season was spent racing in Italy's Formula

ANOTHER NEW FACE: Enrique is the latest from racing's land of plenty

TRACK NOTES

Nationality	BRAZILIAN
Born	OCTOBER 19, 1978, CURITIBA, BRAZIL
Teams	PROST 2001?

CAREER RECORD

First Grand Prix	2001 AUSTRALIAN GP
Starts	NONE
Wins	NONE
Pole positions	NONE
Fastest laps	NONE
Points	NONE
Honours	1986 EUROPEAN FORMULA RENAULT CHAMPION; 1991 & 1990 BRAZILIAN KARTING CHAMPION; 1989 SAO PAULO KARTING CHAMPION

Europa Boxer series, when he ended the year an impressive fourth overall, with a race win to his name. Moving up to the European Formula Renault series in 1996, Enrique dominated for the works Tatuus team, scoring almost twice the points tally of his closest rival. This landed him a ride in British Formula Three with Promatecme. Despite winning at Spa, he was overshadowed by his team-mate Nicolas Minassian and ended up fifth overall. Staying on in 1998, Enrique improved to second, but won just once from the last 10 rounds. Chastened, Enrique headed for Formula 3000 in 1999, joining the RSM Marko-run Red Bull Junior team. Here he was expected to shine, but failed even to qualify for the final two rounds and his best result was a fifth. There had been sufficient flashes of speed, though, for a second season and Enrique qualified on pole in Spain. Yet his form was patchy and fourth at Silverstone was his best as he ranked 15th. In close-season testing for 2001, though, Enrique consistently topped the time sheets. But, his aim was set on a loftier target.

*This driver for this team was provisional at the time of going to press and had not been confirmed

TIPS FOR THE TOP

Jenson Button proved last year that it's really worth looking to the junior formulae to spot the stars of the future. So, along came Kimi Raikkonen and landed a Formula One ride for this year with even less experience. Here are the ones to watch for the future.

I WONDER... : Flying Scot Dario Franchitti ponders what might have been if he hadn't quit Europe to race in ChampCars

The accepted route into a Formula One ride is for a driver to spend his or her childhood racing karts, graduate to Formula Ford, then to a junior slicks and wings category such as Formula Renault, then to cars of greater technical sophistication with a spell in Formula Three before learning how to handle more power on the Grand Prix circuits around Europe in Formula 3000. The final jump to Formula One is the hardest to make, with the fewest openings at which to aim. Some are able only to get their foot in the door with a Formula One team by signing up to be its test driver. This may not be a racing seat, but it offers invaluable mileage in a Formula One car and a chance to learn to understand the facets that are so important for wringing those vital last fractions of a second out of the car. However, not all test drivers make that final move into a team's racing line-up. So there are a lot of frustrated drivers with strong Formula 3000 records out there unable to break into Formula One.

Imagine, then, how their frustration must have been compounded at the start of last year when a driver who had finished only third in the previous year's British Formula Three Championship and had never raced in Formula 3000 leapt past them all and landed a plum Formula One racing seat with Williams. Step forward Jenson Button. That he then went on to shine on the sport's toughest stage rather weakened the currency of their hard-earned Formula 3000 successes, especially as it has encouraged top teams to look back to the junior formulae for their stars of the future, with drivers only just starting in Formula Three already inking long-term deals with Formula One teams. Talent, you see, is something that drivers either have or don't have, and the top teams all want to spot it, snap it up and train it.

But then Button's meteoric rise to Formula One was put in the shade last November when Sauber signed a driver with even less car-racing experience: Kimi Raikkonen. The Finn had contested just 23 car races in all and hadn't as much as sat in a Formula Three car, graduating instead from the category below: Formula Renault. The FIA thought long and hard about giving him the superlicence required to compete in Formula Onc, and the months ahead will

Only Jacques Villeneuve and Alessandro Zanardi have made the journey in recent years, being followed this year by Juan Pablo Montoya, who is hoping to prove with Williams that predecessor Zanardi's poor form on his return was not typical.

Third in Formula 3000 last year was Mark Webber, winner of the Silverstone round. He tested for Arrows in 2000 before signing a test deal with Benetton. He will also contest a second season of Formula 3000 this year, and Australia is desperate to have a Grand Prix driver of its own to go with its excellent Grand Prix, so Mark could be just that man. Mind you, a compatriot by the name of James Courtney is moving up to Formula Three after cleaning up in last year's British Formula Ford Championship, so Mark had better keep on his toes.

Once linked with Ferrari, Spanish teenager Fernando Alonso now looks set to be driving for Minardi. He won once in last year's Formula 3000, at Spa-Francorchamps, as well as showing excellent form elsewhere, so attracting the attention of Minardi, with whom he enjoyed a few tests during the 2000 World Championship.

Only one other driver won Formula 3000 races in 2000, with Tomas Enge triumphing in a wet/dry race at Hockenheim. However, last year's Jordan test driver was too erratic to sustain a challenge, and this was his only podium visit. His team-mate in the second half of the year was Tomas Scheckter, the runner-up in the British Formula Three Championship finishing second behind Enge on the team's day of days at Hockenheim. Showing all the skills of his World Champion father Jody, he has opted to concentrate on testing for Jaguar this year, with a few races being undertaken only to keep his hand in.

There were no British winners in Formula 3000, although Darren Manning, Jamie Davies and Justin Wilson all claimed a second place apiece, with Wilson the most consistent of the trio for Nordic Racing. As the youngest of the three, he has the most chance of graduating to the big time, although Manning has strong links with BAR, for whom he tested a great deal last year.

One more driver who shone last year in Formula 3000 and is worth keeping an eye on is Sebastien Bourdais, the frail-looking French driver possessing good natural speed, as shown by his second place at Magny-Cours.

The driver who is set to challenge the likes of Bourdais in Formula 3000 this year is Antonio Pizzonia, who fought at the front of the British Formula Three series last year with Scheckter, and French Formula Three

A CHIP OFF THE OLD BLOCK?: Tomas Scheckter has displayed all the speed of his World Champion father Jody. He's already Jaguar's test driver

prove whether they were right or wrong in waiving their previous stipulations that required a driver at least to have raced in Formula Three.

THE QUICK ONES

Before looking straight to racing's kindergarten for the stars of the future, there are a few drivers in Formula 3000 who shouldn't be overlooked. First among these ought to be last year's champion Bruno Junqueira – the

driver who was pipped by Button for that number-two seat at Williams last year – and the driver he edged out at the final round, Nicolas Minassian. The Frenchman won three times for the Super Nova team, but Brazilian Junqueira won one more for the sister Petrobras Junior team. Neither, however, is heading to Formula One, as both have opted instead for race seats in the ChampCar series. Whether they cross back over the great divide remains to be seen, but few leap from ChampCars to Formula One.

Champion Jonathan Cochet. Wealthy Brazilian Pizzonia ended up as champion, but he appeared to lose his way mid-season when he was testing for Benetton, before bouncing back with his fifth win to claim the title. He has the speed and simply needs the focus this year to win at this higher level. The French Formula Three Championship is often overlooked as it dwindled through the 1990s, but Cochet also won the international invitation Marlboro Masters race at Zandvoort, beating the best of all the other Formula Three series, save for those racing in Germany who had a race of their own that weekend. Ignore him at your peril.

ON THE UP: Brazilian ace Antonio Pizzonia stormed to last year's British Formula Three title and wants more

THE NEXT BRIT?: Darren Manning starred in Formula 3000 last year and tested for BAR. He deserves a shot at Formula One

Giorgio Pantano and Andre Lotterer are graduating to Formula 3000 from German Formula Three, with Vitor Meira arriving as the South American Formula Three champion. Lotterer was snapped up early last year on a long-term contract with Jaguar.

Looking further afield for drivers who might shine in Formula One in the future, two drivers have been impressing on the North American racing scene. They are New Zealander Scott Dixon, who starred in last year's Indy Lights series, while Briton Dan Wheldon ended the year as top rookie in Toyota Atlantic, finishing runner-up overall.

However, both are likely to focus on ChampCars. With the relative equality of equipment as the majority of teams field either Reynard or Lola chassis, thus offering a superior chance of running near the front, you can't blame them.

TEST DRIVING

The image of the test driver was changed last year by the fact that it became seen as a route for a Formula One driver to redirect his career, as a sort of pit stop before rejoining the race in better shape than before.

Take Olivier Panis, who had spent his entire Formula One career from 1994 with Ligier and then Prost after the team changed its name. However, the team lost direction and so seemingly did Olivier. McLaren coaxed him to give up offers of race seats with tail-end teams. Instead, McLaren wanted to harness his Formula One racing experience in its test team. So Olivier disappeared from the limelight that preserves the careers of the top drivers, but instead found himself in what was probably the best car, with the added advantage of being able to compare himself with double World Champion Mika Hakkinen and David Coulthard. So good was his form that BAR snapped up Olivier for one of its race seats for 2001, putting him in a far stronger position than he would have been in had he raced on with Prost.

With this in mind, Alexander Wurz and Ricardo Zonta have chosen to take this route with a view to bouncing back into a race seat for 2002. In fact, Zonta was replaced by Panis, and after talks with tail-end teams elected to follow suit; he is going to spend this year with Jordan, testing in support of Heinz-Harald Frentzen and Jarno Trulli – two drivers he'll be looking to compare favourably against. Likewise, Wurz lost his ride at Benetton and was courted by McLaren to fill the role vacated by Panis. The Austrian is one of the more technically-minded drivers and will most likely bloom away from the volatile atmosphere of driving for a team run by the effervescent but unpredictable Flavio Briatore.

Another driver with years of Formula One racing experience behind him who will spend 2001 pounding around the test circuits, but not racing, is Mika Salo. However, he at least is assured a race seat for 2002 as he will be heading Toyota's attack. Alongside him for this year is Allan McNish, a driver who spent years testing for Benetton and McLaren before turning to sportscar racing when no race seats were made available. Should he land a race seat with Toyota for 2002, it will be 12 years after he was runner-up to David Brabham in British Formula Three.

Stepping back to go forwards isn't something being done only by drivers downgrading to a test seat, as former Tyrrell and Arrows racer Toranosuke Takagi elected to return to Formula Nippon – Japan's version of Formula 3000 – for 2000. Runner-up in the series in 1995, he shone as never before to walk off with the title with eight wins from 10 starts. Toranosuke has opted to take another detour: he has ditched longtime backer Honda and teamed up with Toyota. This isn't as part of its embryonic Formula One team, rather as a driver for the Toyota-powered Walker Racing ChampCar team. Should he impress, then he might be considered for 2002.

AUSTRALIA EXPECTS: Mark Webber is the driver tipped to put Australia back on the Formula One map. It has been a generation since their last World Champion, in 1980

IT'S THE LAW...

The FIA has introduced a number of safety-driven rule changes for 2001. As in previous years, many of these modifications and refinements remain hidden and may not be immediately obvious to the untrained eye

MAIN RULE CHANGES FOR 2001...

A	Front wing raised 50mm	
B	Double wheel tethers	
C	25mm thick padding added to protect driver's legs	
D	Universal seat mountings	
E	Cockpit enlarged and moved further back from front wheels	
F	Roll bar test more stringent (four times more force than 2000)	
G	External chassis dimensions increased	

ON THE LIMIT...

The pit lane speed limiter is a vital 'tool' for the drivers. Exceeding the 80km/h speed limit during the race carries an inevitably disastrous 10-second stop-go penalty

Limiter effect is controlled only by car's speed, as detected by sensors on front wheels (H). Car's fuel flap (I) must open and rear light (J) must flash when limiter is activated.
Drivers use button on steering wheel to activate limiter on entry to pit lane to control speed. Releasing it on exit restores full power

DOUBLE STANDARDS

Wheel tethers are to be 'doubled up' for 2001. 'Anchored' to each wheel and internally, on suspension mountings, each cable has a breaking strength of five tonnes – the equivalent of five small cars!
Cables run through the centre of the suspension arms. Any failure of the suspension means that wheel can move, in an arc, only around the cable's length

Graphic © Russell Lewis

B
Anchor point
Forward wishbone
8mm Kevlar cable

CAR DIMENSIONS

Car dimensions *(shown in mm)* and weight are subject to strict limits

Mandatory on-board camera mounting positions

Average (unrestricted): **4400**
Max: 1800
Max: 1000
Max: 1400
Max: 1400
Max overall height: **950**

Bodywork size, restriction and positioning rules are highly complex. Illustration shows main overall sizes only.

BENDING RULES...

Two types of test – impact, or crash testing, and static load application – are carried out on specific areas of the car to check strength, deformation and deceleration characteristics.

Cockpit test areas:
(1) **Rear roll-hoop** *(combined test for vertical, lateral and longitudinal stress)*;
(2) **Cockpit rim**; (3) **Steering column**; (4) **Forward roll-hoop**;
(5)/(6) **Cockpit sides**;
(7) **Fuel tank floor**

F1 cockpit cross-section

Static load test

Impact test

THE RIGHT CHOICE...

Teams will have ten sets of tyres available over each GP weekend, of which only seven – all of the same compound – may be used for Saturday and Sunday sessions

QUAL
10-3

Wheel balancing
A restriction on front wheel width now applies specific regulation limits to both front and rear wheels. *(Dimensions refer to wheel with fully inflated tyre)*

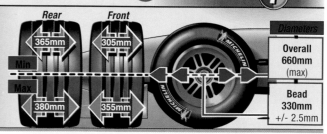

Rear
Front
365mm
305mm
Min
Max
380mm
355mm

Diameters
Overall 660mm (max)
Bead 330mm +/- 2.5mm

A DAY AT THE RACES...

It's Sunday morning and all roads lead to the race track. For the tens of thousands that will pack the circuit perimeter, the most stressful aspect of today will probably amount to little more than keeping the beer cool and the bugs off the sandwiches! For the 'chosen few' strapped into their racing machines on the starting grid the shape of race-day is a just a bit more urgent. Take a trip with Ralf Schumacher from wake-up to a wheel-spinning Grand Prix 'go'!

GET ME TO THE GRID ON TIME

11:00 FIA drivers' briefing

Debriefing with engineers to decide final race plan

10:15

09:00 Puts on overalls. *Warm-up session begins at 9:30am*

08:00 Meeting with engineers to discuss any changes made to the car over Saturday night

07:30 **Breakfast:** specially prepared muesli with yoghurt

07:00 Leave hotel for circuit

06:30 **Alarm call**

11:30 Drivers' parade

12:00 Rest

12:45 Massage

13:15

14:00

1 **Leave pits for starting grid:** once on the grid, holds final discussions with engineers and – in common with most drivers at this stage – drinks 'lots' of water

Formation lap: looks for any changes in track surface or conditions, at the same time, attempting to get as much heat as possible into tyres and brakes. When back in starting position checks to see that other cars have stopped

-0:00:05

Five seconds to go... and the critical moment as the first set of red lights comes. 100% concentration must now remain balanced between watching the lights and maintaining optimum engine revs

-0:00:04

-0:00:03

-0:00:02

-0:00:01

One second to go... *All five sets of red lights are on. With engines screaming all around him, driver's focus is 100% on 'lights out'*

-0:00:00

GO!... *The lights go out and the charge for the first corner is on. As cars accelerate to 100mph in around three seconds, a split-second can make or break a weekend's work...*

FIVE STEPS TO TURN ONE...

The lights go out and 'all-round' concentration becomes the key

1) Priority is to get away cleanly, controlling wheel-spin and getting the power down smoothly

2) Look for the car ahead of you and go for any 'gaps' in the field – left or right

3) You must be alert to all of the cars around you, defending your own position to avoid losing any places

4) 'Claim' your position and steady the car;

5) Now you must look for 'turn one' and find enough road for a clean run through

Mirror, mirror... They may look too small to be of much use, but in the critical opening stages of a race, a driver's mirrors can prove a major asset!

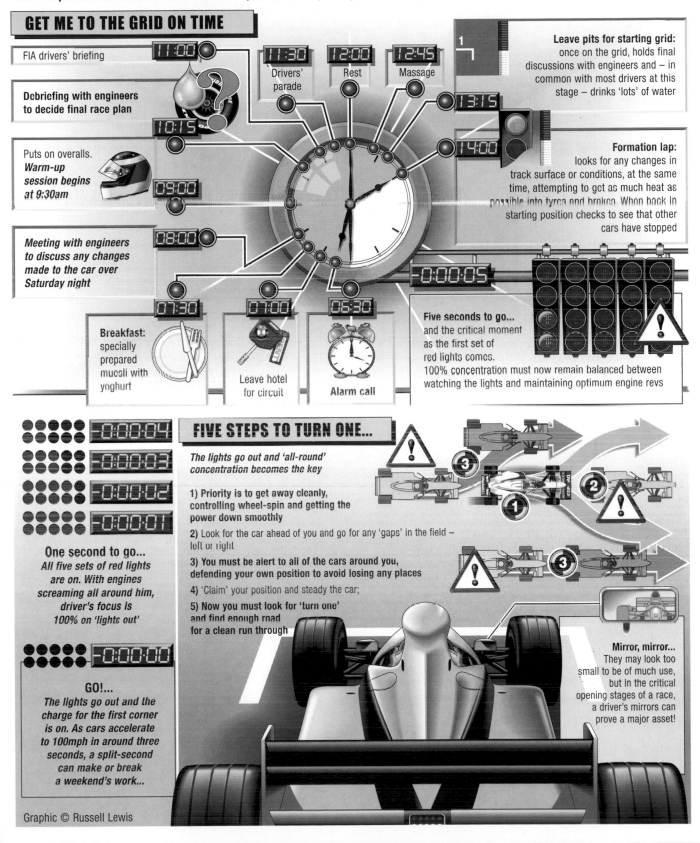

Graphic © Russell Lewis

SAFETY FIRST...

When chaos visits the racetrack, the track Formula 1 safety car can be a key player. Sudden, heavy rainfall, accidents that block or 'litter' the track or other unforseen problems, can all bring the high-powered silver Mercedes Safety Car into play.

SAFETY CAR SPECIFICATIONS

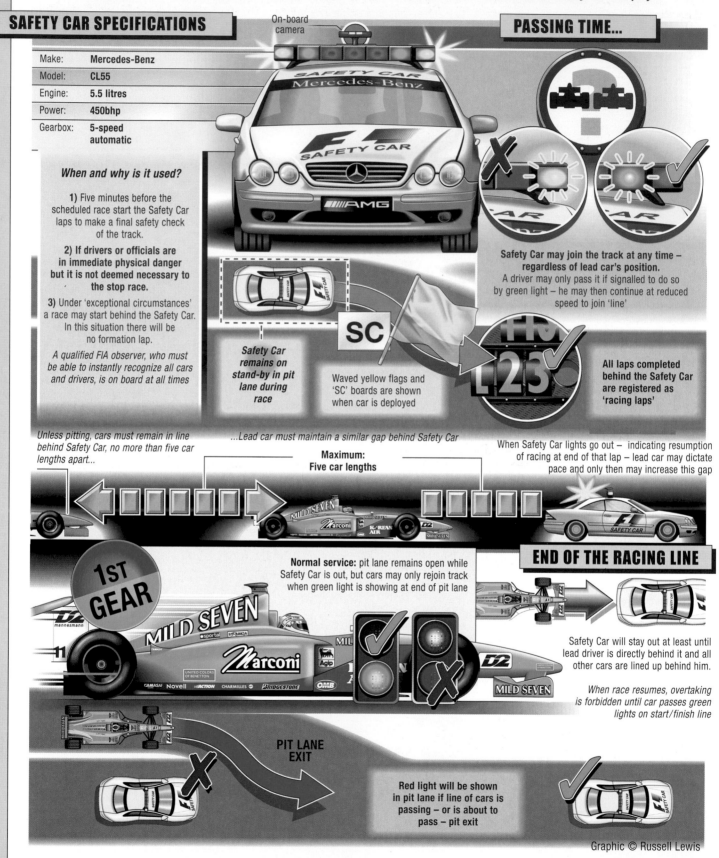

On-board camera

Make:	Mercedes-Benz
Model:	CL55
Engine:	5.5 litres
Power:	450bhp
Gearbox:	5-speed automatic

When and why is it used?

1) Five minutes before the scheduled race start the Safety Car laps to make a final safety check of the track.

2) If drivers or officials are in immediate physical danger but it is not deemed necessary to the stop race.

3) Under 'exceptional circumstances' a race may start behind the Safety Car. In this situation there will be no formation lap.

A qualified FIA observer, who must be able to instantly recognize all cars and drivers, is on board at all times

Safety Car remains on stand-by in pit lane during race

Waved yellow flags and 'SC' boards are shown when car is deployed

PASSING TIME...

Safety Car may join the track at any time – regardless of lead car's position.
A driver may only pass it if signalled to do so by green light – he may then continue at reduced speed to join 'line'

All laps completed behind the Safety Car are registered as 'racing laps'

Unless pitting, cars must remain in line behind Safety Car, no more than five car lengths apart...

...Lead car must maintain a similar gap behind Safety Car

When Safety Car lights go out – indicating resumption of racing at end of that lap – lead car may dictate pace and only then may increase this gap

Maximum: Five car lengths

1ST GEAR

Normal service: pit lane remains open while Safety Car is out, but cars may only rejoin track when green light is showing at end of pit lane

END OF THE RACING LINE

Safety Car will stay out at least until lead driver is directly behind it and all other cars are lined up behind him.

When race resumes, overtaking is forbidden until car passes green lights on start/finish line

PIT LANE EXIT

Red light will be shown in pit lane if line of cars is passing – or is about to pass – pit exit

Graphic © Russell Lewis

THE MEASURE OF SUCCESS...

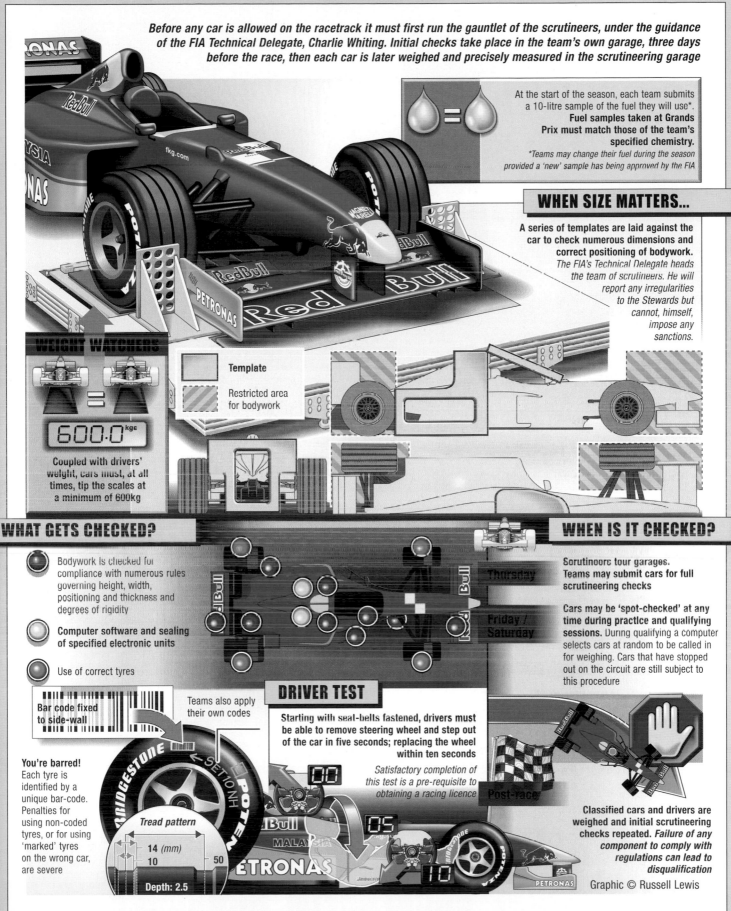

Before any car is allowed on the racetrack it must first run the gauntlet of the scrutineers, under the guidance of the FIA Technical Delegate, Charlie Whiting. Initial checks take place in the team's own garage, three days before the race, then each car is later weighed and precisely measured in the scrutineering garage

At the start of the season, each team submits a 10-litre sample of the fuel they will use*. **Fuel samples taken at Grands Prix must match those of the team's specified chemistry.** *Teams may change their fuel during the season provided a 'new' sample has being approved by the FIA*

WHEN SIZE MATTERS...

A series of templates are laid against the car to check numerous dimensions and **correct positioning of bodywork.** *The FIA's Technical Delegate heads the team of scrutineers. He will report any irregularities to the Stewards but cannot, himself, impose any sanctions.*

WEIGHT WATCHERS

= 600·0 kgs

Coupled with drivers' weight, cars must, at all times, tip the scales at a minimum of 600kg

- Template
- Restricted area for bodywork

WHAT GETS CHECKED?

- Bodywork is checked for compliance with numerous rules governing height, width, positioning and thickness and degrees of rigidity
- **Computer software and sealing of specified electronic units**
- Use of correct tyres

Bar code fixed to side-wall

Teams also apply their own codes

You're barred! Each tyre is identified by a unique bar-code. Penalties for using non-coded tyres, or for using 'marked' tyres on the wrong car, are severe

Tread pattern
14 (mm)
10   50
Depth: 2.5

DRIVER TEST

Starting with seat-belts fastened, drivers must be able to remove steering wheel and step out of the car in five seconds; replacing the wheel within ten seconds

Satisfactory completion of this test is a pre-requisite to obtaining a racing licence

WHEN IS IT CHECKED?

Scrutineers tour garages. Teams may submit cars for full scrutineering checks

Thursday

Cars may be 'spot-checked' at any time during practice and qualifying sessions. During qualifying a computer selects cars at random to be called in for weighing. Cars that have stopped out on the circuit are still subject to this procedure

Friday / Saturday

Post-race

Classified cars and drivers are weighed and initial scrutineering checks repeated. *Failure of any component to comply with regulations can lead to disqualification*

Graphic © Russell Lewis

Some love Monaco, others plump for Spa-Francorchamps and most British fans still have a soft spot for Silverstone, but one of the greatest features of the World Championship is that it's held on circuits of infinite variety. No two circuits are the same, with some favouring certain cars and others offering their rivals a chance. Equally, some drivers produce their best performances on the twists and turns of Monaco and the Hungaroring, while others go for gold on the high-speed straights of Monza and Hockenheim. There's a new challenge every fortnight.

Everyone – from team owner to designer to driver – has a favourite circuit, but one of the greatest challenges comes when the World Championship visits a circuit for the first time. In 1999, that was Malaysia's all-new Sepang circuit and last year it was the special circuit on the banking and around the infield at the Indianapolis Motor Speedway. The teams use computer modelling so they can guess what set-up their cars should run, and thus waste little time when they arrive for the Grand Prix. So it's an extra pressure for all concerned, but it does make for an extra treat for the race fans, allowing them to watch the drivers do battle on pastures new, swap a few of the old circuits for ones that are made to be more suitable for racing action.

The variety of circuits is huge, from the twisty circuit around the streets of Monaco to the flat and wide-open spaces of Silverstone to the flat-out blasts through the forests at Hockenheim and the technical twists of Suzuka. And this is how Formula One should be, forcing

MELBOURNE SEPANG INTERLAGOS IMOLA BARCELONA SILVERSTONE HOCKENHEIM HUNGARORING SP

BIRD'S EYE VIEW: David Coulthard's McLaren is seen from above as it blasts out of the tunnel at Monaco and approaches the chicane

the drivers to prove to everyone that they are the best in the world on as many different types of circuit as possible.

A visit to a circuit isn't only about the racing surface, however, as another factor in the overall experience is the particular atmosphere of the venue supplied by the local fans. After all, there's no way that the screaming crowds in Brazil could be compared to the thousands who pack the grandstands in Germany. All they have in common is a love of Formula One, but their way of showing this comes from opposite ends of the spectrum: a carnival versus a bierfest. Less passionate about the racing are the crowds in Monaco, many of whom are perhaps more interested in potential business contacts. Nevertheless, the Monaco Grand Prix remains one that everyone should attend, to marvel at the narrowness of the streets and the glitziness of those fortunate enough to be invited on board the yachts in the harbour or while away their evenings in the casino. Then, of course, there are the American fans,

welcomed back in hundreds of thousands last autumn when Formula One regained a foothold in the United States. No-one celebrates a sporting event in the way Americans do.

There are no new circuits joining the World Championship calendar in 2001, but already some of the more recent additions feel like part of the furniture, and none more so than Melbourne, home of the Australian Grand Prix since 1996. This is a city not only equipped with a great track just a short tram ride from its centre, but one that embraces any sporting event with a passion seldom matched elsewhere in the world. Cricket and Australian Rules football are their bread and butter, but Formula One caught on in no time, with the organizers deserving praise for the fulsome package of races and events that pack their support programme like nowhere else, taking over the mantle from the British Grand Prix in offering

the most bangs for the spectators' buck.

With Ferrari being the most popular team, red flags are waved on the spectator banks of every circuit, but nowhere are so many seen as in the two races held in Italy – at Imola and Monza. For these are the homes of the tifosi, the Ferrari fans. Monza may have chicanes breaking its flow, but the circuit is cloaked in a wonderful feeling of its history.

Likewise, the Nurburgring used today is not a patch on the original version that was used until Niki Lauda was nearly killed when he crashed there in 1976, but visitors need only visit the circuit museum to comprehend what drivers experienced in the early days when the lap was fully 14 miles long.

So, 17 Grands Prix, 17 very different circuits and 17 totally individual and passionate crowds. No wonder Formula One is such an exciting and cosmopolitan sport.

NG MONACO MONTREAL NURBURGRING MAGNY-COURS
ANCORCHAMPS MONZA INDIANAPOLIS SUZUKA

MELBOURNE

ROUND 1: MARCH 4, 2001

McLaren must wonder what it has to do to finish the Australian GP after two years of domination led to nothing. Ferrari, on the other hand, will be looking to make it three in a row at Melbourne.

HERO OF THE TRACK

From the neighbouring state of New South Wales, Jack Brabham headed for England in the mid-1950s and was able to profit from Cooper introducing revolutionary rear-engined cars with which he won the world title in 1959 and 1960. A change of rules saw Brabham enjoy the best engine as he won his third title in 1966, this time in a car of his own construction. He later sold the Brabham team and focussed on the careers of his three racing sons.

FLAT-OUT BLAST: Mika Hakkinen has always flown at Melbourne, but he hasn't scored there since 1998

Considering Australia's exceptional sporting pedigree, it is strange how Formula One – with the marked exception of three-times World Champion Jack Brabham and Alan Jones – has largely passed it by. Cricketers, rugby players, track athletes and swimmers have all excelled, but perhaps the reason for Australia's dearth of top-line drivers lies in the fact that those who have made it have had to do so by turning their backs on their homeland and head to Europe to pit their skills in the junior formulae. Brabham and the trickle of hopefuls who followed him didn't have the help of the best shop window of all: a home Grand Prix. However, after

hosting non-championship Grands Prix, usually for non-Formula One cars, Australia joined the World Championship in 1985. It was the streets of Adelaide that opened their arms to Formula One, with this race seldom failing to provide high excitement, helped by the fact it was the final race of the year.

Who can forget the race in 1986 when it all went wrong for Nigel Mansell in the most spectacular fashion? The title was a three-way battle between Mansell, his Williams team-mate Nelson Piquet and McLaren's Alain Prost. And, with Mansell heading for the title, he had a monster blow-out, leaving Prost to win the race and the title.

The race was stopped almost before it had started in 1989 because torrential rain had caused many of the cars to aquaplane into the walls. Amazingly for a country that is predominantly arid, rain hit again in 1991.

The 1994 World Championship showdown between Michael Schumacher and Damon Hill will never be forgotten, as Schumacher's leading Benetton clipped one of the surrounding walls. Just as Hill tried to dive by, Schumacher moved across and they collided. Schumacher was pitched off, but Hill was unable to continue, his Williams limping off with damaged suspension. And so Schumacher became champion.

CHANGING STATES

The state of Victoria is the home of the Australian motorsport industry, so it was only right that its capital, Melbourne, should take over the Grand Prix. It did so in 1996, as the season-opener. And it almost provided one of the biggest shocks ever as Jacques Villeneuve was heading for victory on his debut (only achieved previously by Giancarlo Baghetti in 1961) before his oil pressure dropped and Williams team-mate Hill won.

Villeneuve looked set to gain revenge in 1997 after dominating qualifying, but Eddie Irvine took him out at the first corner, and so David Coulthard was able to race to McLaren's first win since Adelaide in 1993, with Heinz-Harald Frentzen crashing out of second in the closing laps.

Unlike Adelaide's street circuit, Melbourne's Albert Park circuit is all in a park. Running clockwise around a lake, the circuit begins with an ess that's approached at 180mph leading on to the second-gear right-hander where Martin Brundle flipped in 1996. The track bends right and the drivers hit fifth before a second-gear chicane, sixth and 170mph before another ess. Into the back section of the circuit, sweeping left, drivers see 180mph as they negotiate two rights around the far end of the lake before then completing the lap with a slow, second-gear left-hander and a quicker right.

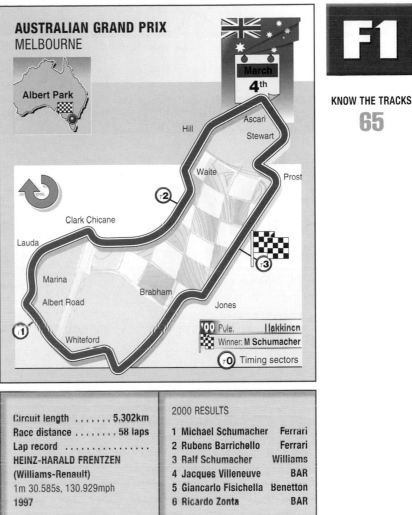

AUSTRALIAN GRAND PRIX
MELBOURNE

Albert Park

March 4th

Ascari · Stewart · Prost · Hill · Waite · Clark Chicane · Lauda · Marina · Albert Road · Whiteford · Brabham · Jones

'00 Pole, Hakkinen
Winner: M Schumacher
Timing sectors

Circuit length 5.302km	
Race distance . . . . 58 laps	
Lap record	
HEINZ-HARALD FRENTZEN	
(Williams-Renault)	
1m 30.585s, 130.929mph	
1997	

2000 RESULTS

1	Michael Schumacher	Ferrari
2	Rubens Barrichello	Ferrari
3	Ralf Schumacher	Williams
4	Jacques Villeneuve	BAR
5	Giancarlo Fisichella	Benetton
6	Ricardo Zonta	BAR

McLAREN'S HIGHS AND LOWS

The 1998 race marked the start of McLaren's dominant year, with Hakkinen and Coulthard leaving the opposition in their wake. But even winning by such a large margin left a bad taste, as Hakkinen thought he'd been called into the pits and lost the lead. Coulthard stuck to an agreement that whoever entered the first corner ahead would win the race, and so he slowed and let Hakkinen by with three laps to go to win. Third-placed Frentzen was fully a lap down in his Williams.

McLaren dominated again in 1999, but both drivers retired. With Michael Schumacher having had to start from the back of the grid, this left the way clear for Eddie Irvine to score his first win for Ferrari ahead of Jordan's Frentzen and Ralf Schumacher's Williams.

Last year, McLaren's duo ran away in the lead again for the third year in a row. But again Coulthard dropped out, followed by Hakkinen, and this left Michael Schumacher leading from Frentzen. But the Jordan driver had a delayed pit-stop and fell back behind Rubens Barrichello and Ralf Schumacher, after which his gearbox failed, with Williams' engine supplier BMW delighted by a podium finish on their return to the sport. After a debut year without points, BAR enjoyed both drivers scoring, with Jacques Villeneuve fourth and Ricardo Zonta sixth.

MELBOURNE CITYSCAPE: This aerial view down to the Clark Chicane shows off Melbourne's downtown

SEPANG

ROUND 2: MARCH 18, 2001

With facilities more modern than at any circuit in the world, Sepang is one of the shining lights in the World Championship calendar, but its soaring temperatures and humidity take the edge off its appeal to those working there.

FIA president Max Mosley spent much of last year denigrating Silverstone for offering facilities that he no longer thought sufficiently modern for Formula One. When he cited an example of contemporary excellence, he pointed to Sepang, the circuit that was built from scratch near the capital of Kuala Lumpur thanks to full backing from the Malaysian government. In Sepang, it built itself a state-of-the-art racing facility, demonstrating the advantage of starting with a clean sheet rather than modifying an existing venue. Sepang is how the FIA would like all circuits to be developed as plans to spread the gospel of Formula One ever wider are pursued.

SMOOTH AND WIDE

The key to Sepang's popularity is that its racing surface is both smooth and wide. It also offers a couple of long straights, a good mixture of corners, brand-new pit facilities and excellent access, so it's no wonder that teams like going there. Impressively, with Sepang built on level ground, spectators in the giant main grandstand can see to the far ends of the circuit.

A lap begins when the start/finish straight turns sharply right, forcing drivers to haul their cars down from 185mph to 50mph. The track feeds almost immediately into a left-hand hairpin, where David Coulthard sprung a surprise in 1999 to catch Michael Schumacher off-guard. This sequence proves a squeeze on the opening lap, with Pedro Diniz, Nick Heidfeld and Pedro de la Rosa clashing last year. Opening out, the track turns through a long right-hander, with drivers hitting 180mph before slowing for a tight right-hander where Johnny Herbert was pitched off last year. This is followed by a long left then an open, sixth-gear right and two fourth-gear rights onto a short straight into a left-hand hairpin. A pair of right-handers follows, then a fifth-gear left before a long right. The back straight is long enough to allow slipstreaming and wide enough into the final corner – a left-hand hairpin – for drivers to overtake. Even if this move doesn't work, as long as they emerge on the tail of the car ahead, they have another chance for slipstreaming down the even longer start/finish straight.

MAKING THEIR OWN HISTORY

Malaysia doesn't have the rich motorsport history of Britain, France or Italy. It started by holding races on street circuits at Johore Batu and Penang only in the 1960s. A permanent facility called Shah Alam was built in 1968 near Kuala Lumpur. This hosted a round of the Sportscar World Championship in 1985, but wasn't a success. Malaysia's national racing scene improved in the 1990s as South-East Asia developed a motor-racing network of its own, but plans for Malaysia to

A FAMOUS PROFILE: The roof of the grandstand against a glorious sunset

LIGHTS OUT, ACTION: The McLarens lead the field down to the first corner, but they weren't to go on and win the race

host a Grand Prix were hit when the South-East Asian economy slumped. However, they went ahead and built Sepang, and it was launched early in 1999 by a round of the Motorcycle World Championship.

Formula One's first visit marked Michael Schumacher's comeback from a broken leg, and he obstructed Mika Hakkinen's McLaren to help team-mate Eddie Irvine escape to win. The Ferraris were then thrown out for an alleged technical irregularity and it was a week before Ferrari was handed its points back, meaning that Hakkinen hadn't clinched the world title after all and would have to race for it in the final round of the Championship. History relates that Hakkinen settled the matter at Suzuka.

Hakkinen's hopes of winning last year were scuppered when he jumped the start and his stop-go penalty dropped him to 18th. This left Coulthard in front, but it soon became clear that Schumacher was on a one-stop strategy, while the McLaren driver had started light on fuel and would be pitting twice. Schumacher changed to a two-stop strategy after an unusually early stop by Coulthard to clear debris from a sidepod that was causing overheating; he emerged in front, and was just able to resist Coulthard to the flag.

This year, the Malaysian Grand Prix will be second on the World Championship calendar rather than holding the season-closer. Whether this fills the grandstands remains to be seen, for there were spaces aplenty on the spectator banking last year – and this for the round that was expected to be a championship shoot-out. Sure, Schumacher had claimed the title a fortnight earlier at Suzuka, but if you've bought a ticket, you don't stay at home just because you know the identity of the champion.

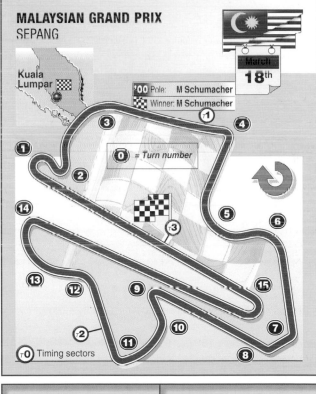

MALAYSIAN GRAND PRIX
SEPANG

Kuala Lumpar

March 18th

'00 Pole: M Schumacher
Winner: M Schumacher

⓪ = Turn number

⓪ Timing sectors

Circuit length 5.542km	**2000 RESULTS**
Race distance . . . . 56 laps	1 Michael Schumacher Ferrari
Lap record	2 David Coulthard McLaren
MIKA HAKKINEN	3 Rubens Barrichello Ferrari
(McLaren-Mercedes)	4 Mika Hakkinen McLaren
1m 38.543s, 125.832mph	5 Jacques Villeneuve BAR
2000	6 Eddie Irvine Jaguar

INTERLAGOS

ROUND 3: APRIL 1, 2001

One of the great, traditional circuits remaining on the Formula One calendar, Interlagos offers some wonderful corners and a party atmosphere that would erupt if a Brazilian driver were to win on home ground.

HERO OF THE TRACK

Rubens Barrichello has a massive shadow out of which to emerge – that of the late Ayrton Senna. He has admitted that this has been a struggle, but his 1999 and 2000 visits had the crowd cheering him on when he led the race for Stewart in the first of these years and then led briefly for Ferrari last year. Neither race yielded the win he so craves, but it could be very different in 2001.

ROUND THE BEND: Not even the start/ finish straight at Interlagos is straight, as it curves uphill past the pits before dipping into Curva 1

Emerson Fittipaldi, Nelson Piquet and Ayrton Senna were drivers who made Brazil proud. For not only did they become World Champions, but they did so several times each, offering Brazil sporting prestige the like of which they have otherwise earned only through football. For all its success, Brazil is thousands of miles from motorsport's axis. It's not just the country's distance from Europe that

highlights the difference, as anyone who visits Interlagos will understand. And it's not just Sao Paulo's soaring temperatures and the poverty of the shanty towns. It's the fact that Brazil is Formula One mad. Not even Europe's liveliest crowd at Imola can match the fervour of those packing the grandstands.

Fittipaldi was the first driver to put the country on the Formula One map, bursting

onto the European racing scene in 1969. After hosting a non-championship race in 1972, Interlagos became home to the Brazilian Grand Prix from 1973, its bowl-like setting magnifying the carnival-style atmosphere.

A lengthy track, with an open section around the perimeter joined to a twisting infield section that ran around a lake, it was a hit with the drivers. Delighting the crowd, Fittipaldi won in 1973 and 1974. Another Brazilian, Carlos Pace, won in 1975. This was to be the last home win until 1983, by which time the race had found a new home.

BRAZILIAN GRAND PRIX
INTERLAGOS

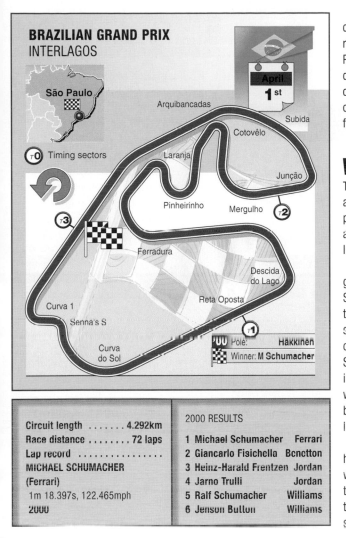

São Paulo

April 1st

Arquibancadas

Subida

Cotovêlo

Laranja

Junção

T0 Timing sectors

Pinheirinho

Mergulho T2

T3

Ferradura

Descida do Lago

Reta Oposta

Curva 1

Senna's S

T1

'00 Pole: Hakkinen

Winner: M Schumacher

Curva do Sol

Circuit length 4.292km	2000 RESULTS		
Race distance .... 72 laps	1 Michael Schumacher	Ferrari
Lap record	2 Giancarlo Fisichella	Benetton
MICHAEL SCHUMACHER	3 Heinz-Harald Frentzen	Jordan
(Ferrari)	4 Jarno Trulli	Jordan
1m 18.397s, 122.465mph	5 Ralf Schumacher	Williams
2000	6 Jenson Button	Williams

character changes as the twisting section starts with a second-gear right-hander that tips the track down to another second-gear corner, Pinheirinho, then up to the even-tighter Bico de Plato. Then it's downhill and up through the gearbox before the last corner, Juncao, out of which drivers hope they can get a good tow all the way uphill onto the pit straight so that they can make a move under braking from 190mph into that first corner.

WINNERS AND LOSERS

The changes to the circuit's layout proved good for the patriotic fans, as Senna finally won on home ground in 1991, sending the extremely partisan crowd berserk. He won there again in 1993, but the atmosphere has never been the same at Interlagos since he died at Imola in 1994.

Since then, it seems that whoever wins the Brazilian Grand Prix goes on to become World Champion, as proved by Michael Schumacher winning at Interlagos in 1994 and 1995, Damon Hill taking the garlands in 1996 and Jacques Villeneuve doing the same in 1997, with Mika Hakkinen dominating proceedings ahead of McLaren team-mate David Coulthard in 1998 as Michael Schumacher had to make do with finishing a further minute back in third. Hakkinen overcame gearbox problems and Schumacher to win again in 1999 after Rubens Barrichello sent the crowd wild by leading in his Stewart. There hadn't been this much excitement at Interlagos since the Senna era.

Last year, Michael Schumacher came away with the spoils, helped by Hakkinen pulling off with oil-pressure problems. Coulthard was second to the finish, but his front wing was found to have been too low. McLaren claimed it had been damaged and swivelled out of true, but the FIA threw him out and Giancarlo Fisichella claimed a surprise second place for Benetton.

Rio de Janeiro relieved Sao Paulo of the race in 1978, hosting the Grand Prix at its Jacarepagua circuit. With two straights joined by several simple corners, and lacking in gradient change, it wasn't as popular as Interlagos, particularly not in that first year when Argentina's Carlos Reutemann beat Brazil's own Fittipaldi. After two years back at Interlagos, Jacarepagua regained the Grand Prix in 1981 and kept it until 1989, with Alain Prost winning five times and Brazilian Piquet twice before Interlagos took over again in 1990.

Interlagos was to prove unrecognizable on their return, as it had been chopped to half its original length, with many of the faster corners made less challenging. Still, some said, that meant there would be half as many bumps per lap on this notoriously corrugated surface.

TESTING GRADIENTS

A lap begins with a dipping left-right that's a nightmare on the first lap, as the cars attempt to funnel through the corner without contact while simultaneously trying to pass those ahead. As a result, there have been some acrobatic shunts there, including a massive one between Gerhard Berger and Michael Andretti in 1993.

Next, the track climbs through the Curva do Sol, a never-ending left-hander onto the long back straight that sees cars hit 185mph before braking hard for Descida do Lago, a tight left-hander that offers the chance for overtaking down the inside. A long climb to the fifth-gear Ferra Dura right-hander follows. Then the track's

TIGHT AND TWISTY: This shot of Cotovelo shows how important it is for cars to put their power down well at Interlagos

IMOLA

ROUND 4: APRIL 15, 2001

Picturesque, testing and surrounded by a parkland setting, Imola has all the right ingredients to be an excellent track. Add to that the fact that its infield and perimeter are packed with the Ferrari-flag-waving *tifosi*, and the combination is a heady one.

HERO OF THE TRACK

It's not often that crowds as passionate as the *tifosi* take anyone other than a Ferrari driver to their hearts. However, one person who has earned their adoration is Ferrari's technical mastermind and tactician, Ross Brawn, whose quick thinking enabled Michael Schumacher to adopt a pit strategy that helped him get in front and stay in front to win both last year's San Marino GP and the one in 1999.

ROUGH TACTICS: Michael Schumacher cuts across on David Coulthard last year

Each of the leading Formula One nations has a Grand Prix every year. Indeed, with the sport's powers trying to move the World Championship away from Europe, many of these nations feel lucky to have held onto theirs. However, both Italy and Germany are blessed with two home Grands Prix per year. Yes, the race at Germany's Nurburgring is known as the European Grand Prix, and this one at Imola is named the San Marino Grand Prix after the nearby principality, but this is a simple case of semantics.

Visit Imola in spring and no Formula One fan could wish to be anywhere else, as the whole place beats with a pulse of excitement. It's great theatre, too, with the Ferrari-mad *tifosi* shouting with delight as their red cars go past, then booing and cat-calling as the grey cars from arch-enemies McLaren try to beat them.

CLIMBING AND FALLING

A lap starts with a blast past the start/finish line, but the Tamburello kink where Senna left the track is chopped and slowed by a chicane that requires second gear rather than sixth... Then it's flat-out down to the Villeneuve corner where Ratzenberger hit the wall, and this has been kinked and slowed, taking the sting out of the entry to Tosa, thus removing one of the year's best overtaking spots, where that combination of a long straight and potential slipstreaming at up to 195mph into a tight corner would see wonderful outbraking manoeuvres.

From the sharp left at Tosa, the track climbs to the Piratella left-hander that crests the wooded hilltop. Then the track dives to the Acque Minerali right-hander before climbing to the chicane at Variante Alta from where it drops to the start line via the double-apex Rivazza left-hander that makes drivers slow from 185mph. The last corner, the Variante Bassa, has been made less extreme as a result of Rubens Barrichello's monster accident there in 1994.

Especially with the slowing effect of the recent chicanes, Imola cooks brakes, wears out tyres and bursts transmissions, leading to a higher-than-average number of retirements.

FERRARI'S FAVOURITE

Built in the 1950s, Imola hit the big time with a non-championship Formula One race in 1963 – won like most races that year by Lotus ace Jim Clark. Key to the growth of the circuit was Enzo Ferrari, who named the circuit after his son Dino who died young; the full name is the Autodromo Enzo e Dino Ferrari. And don't the crowd know it as they fill the banking opposite the final chicane with their flag-waving cast of thousands, cheering the passage of every Ferrari.

Imola feels as though it has held a Grand Prix for ever, but it was only in 1980 that Imola was given the go-ahead, taking over the Italian Grand Prix from Monza for a one-off occasion. That produced a win for Brabham's Nelson Piquet. Since 1981 it has hosted the San Marino Grand Prix, traditionally held early in the season. And Piquet was the winner of the first of these en route to his first World Championship title.

Races here are famous for cars expiring or even running out of fuel in the closing laps, as used to happen when turbocharged engines ruled the roost. However, it's also famous for big shunts, as experienced by Piquet at Tamburello in 1987 and Gerhard Berger at the same corner in 1989. The darkest day for Ferrari fans came in 1991 when Alain Prost spun off on the parade lap, then team-mate Jean Alesi fell off three laps later... Never have the *tifosi* been so shocked and silent.

However, Imola's really terrible weekend came in 1994 when Rubens Barrichello survived a massive accident in practice, but then Roland Ratzenberger didn't in qualifying, and Ayrton Senna crashed inexplicably out of the lead of the race in the Tamburello kink with a fatal outcome. Thus the chicanes that have broken the track's flow.

With memories of 1994 starting to fade, the 1997 race was the best for years, with Jacques Villeneuve, Heinz-Harald Frentzen and Michael Schumacher all leading. Sadly for the *tifosi*, it was Frentzen who took the honours for Williams. Then David Coulthard won in 1998, surviving a scare when an errant plastic bag caught in his radiator and sent his engine temperature soaring, allowing Ferrari's Michael Schumacher to close in. Schumacher won in 1999 after Hakkinen crashed from the lead then Coulthard struggled in traffic. Last year's honours went to Schumacher again, this time after his pit strategy helped him to pass Hakkinen, with Coulthard extricating himself from behind Barrichello when they made their second stops together to claim third position.

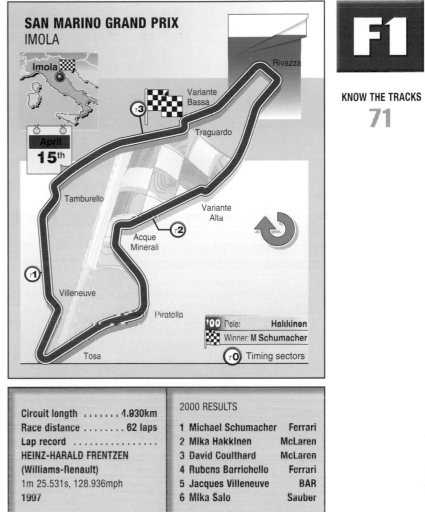

SAN MARINO GRAND PRIX
IMOLA

Imola

April
15th

Rivazza
Variante Bassa
Traguardo
Tamburello
Variante Alta
Acque Minerali
Villeneuve
Piratella
Tosa

100 Pole: **Hakkinen**
Winner: **M Schumacher**
T0 Timing sectors

Circuit length 4.930km	2000 RESULTS
Race distance .... 62 laps	
Lap record	1 Michael Schumacher Ferrari
HEINZ-HARALD FRENTZEN	2 Mika Hakkinen McLaren
(Williams-Renault)	3 David Coulthard McLaren
1m 25.531s, 128.936mph	4 Rubens Barrichello Ferrari
1997	5 Jacques Villeneuve BAR
	6 Mika Salo Sauber

HERO WORSHIP: Michael Schumacher blasts his Ferrari past the adoring *tifosi*, who have eyes only for the Ferrari drivers

BARCELONA

ROUND 5: APRIL 29, 2001

The Spanish Grand Prix has bounced around the country, but Barcelona's Circuit de Catalunya is now well and truly established as its home, and all its passionate fans crave is a home win.

HERO OF THE TRACK

In a country short on Formula One achievement, Pedro de la Rosa could be just the driver to make amends. Starting his third year in Formula One, he has impressed in his two years with Arrows. Technically strong, and a home-town driver too, the crowd will be hoping that his machinery offers him a better shot at glory.

EARLY-SEASON SUN: All the teams test at Barcelona. This is Alexander Wurz pushing his Benetton to its limit last year. This year he will be spending time here for McLaren

Spain has hosted a Grand Prix on and off since 1951, with this honour split between five circuits over the years. The first of these was held at the round-the-houses Pedralbes circuit on the outskirts of Barcelona, with Juan Manuel Fangio triumphant for Alfa Romeo. Mike Hawthorn won for Ferrari on a second visit in 1954, but Spain had to wait until 1968 to host another Grand Prix – this being held on the purpose-built Jarama circuit on the outskirts of Madrid, with Graham Hill winning for Lotus. Yet, a year later, the wonderful Montjuich Park circuit in downtown Barcelona took its turn. These two circuits alternated in holding the Grand Prix until 1975, when the rear wing came off Rolf Stommelen's race-leading Hill at Montjuich Park, and the car was catapulted over the barrier and killed five spectators.

After a final Grand Prix at Jarama in 1981, won famously by Gilles Villeneuve ahead of a train of cars, the Grand Prix then moved to Jerez in 1986. Situated in the heart of the sherry-producing country south of Seville, Jerez is beautifully equipped, but too far from major cities to draw a crowd. Now home mainly to motorbike racing, perhaps its principal claim to fame in years to come will be that it produced the second-closest Grand Prix finish of all time when Ayrton Senna's Lotus edged out Nigel Mansell's Williams by 0.014s in 1986. Another could be when it landed an extra race in 1997, hosting the year's final round when Estoril in neighbouring Portugal failed to complete necessary changes in time; Jacques Villeneuve survived an assault by Michael Schumacher to win the title, letting Mika Hakkinen through on the final lap for his first win. By 1991, though, the Grand Prix had moved north to Barcelona.

start of the climb back up to Banc Sabadell corner. A quick exit from the next two right-handers – fifth-gear corners both – is vital, as they lead onto the main straight. So, a quick exit offers the lap's best opportunity to catch a tow and overtake.

THE RAIN IN SPAIN

Several races here have been marked by heavy rain, and none more so than in 1996 when Michael Schumacher blitzed the field in his Ferrari as many others failed to stay on the track despite circulating at a far more conservative pace as the rain became torrential. Heavy tyre wear was the main feature in 1997, with winner Jacques Villeneuve nursing his Williams along between its two pit stops for fresh Goodyears, while Olivier Panis was able to press far harder on his more resilient Bridgestones as he gave chase. Tyres weren't such an issue in 1998 as the McLarens of Mika Hakkinen and David Coulthard dominated, with Michael Schumacher third and Benetton's Alexander Wurz the only other unlapped runner after their team-mates Eddie Irvine and Giancarlo Fisichella crashed while contesting fourth. The first three were the same again in 1999 in a race notable for Villeneuve propelling his BAR into third and keeping it there until the first pit stops.

Last year's race produced a third consecutive McLaren one-two, but only after Schumacher's Ferrari lost time in the pits and then picked up a puncture.

MIDFIELD TRAFFIC: Mika Salo leads the pack down the hill into the first corner, a tight right/ left sequence

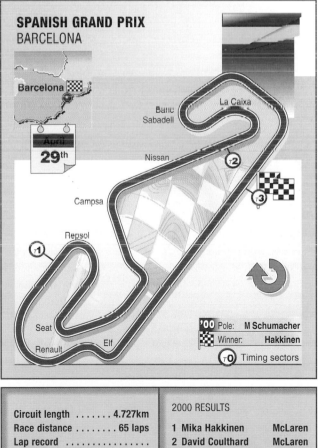

SPANISH GRAND PRIX
BARCELONA

Barcelona

April 29th

Banc Sabadell · La Caixa · Nissan · Campsa · Repsol · Seat · Renault · Elf

'00 Pole: M Schumacher
Winner: Hakkinen
Timing sectors

A HOME, AT LAST

Built for 1991, Barcelona's Catalunya circuit is now the true home of the Spanish Grand Prix. Its layout is better than many other modern circuits in that the lengthy main straight past the pits leads into a sharp right-hand corner that requires heavy braking from 195mph, offering a great possibility for overtaking under braking after the chasing driver has been able to catch a tow from the car ahead and slingshot past. A corner like this sorts the men from the boys, especially late in the race when brakes are past their best, making it a contest of bravery as drivers sit it out to see who will be last onto the pedal.

Elf, the first corner, is a right followed immediately by a left. Then there's a long uphill right-hander. Get this right in fifth gear, and a driver should reach 170mph before hitting the brakes for the Repsol right-hander, from where the track dips and feeds via the Seat left-hander and a left kink into the uphill left-hander that feeds the track up to the Campsa. Cresting the hill at Campsa, the highest point on the circuit, drivers must carry as much speed as possible so that they can hit 185mph before the tight left at La Caixa and the

Circuit length 4.727km	2000 RESULTS	
Race distance . . . . 65 laps	1 Mika Hakkinen	McLaren
Lap record	2 David Coulthard	McLaren
GIANCARLO FISICHELLA	3 Rubens Barrichello	Ferrari
(Jordan-Peugeot)	4 Ralf Schumacher	Williams
1m 22.242s, 128.919mph	5 Michael Schumacher	Ferrari
1997	6 Heinz-Harald Frentzen	Jordan

A1-RING

ROUND 6: MAY 13, 2001

If you want to see the best of the action, buy yourself a grandstand seat by the A1-Ring's first corner. There have been four races since the circuit was built from the Osterreichring, and every one has been a cracker.

HERO OF THE TRACK

Austria's favourite sons Niki Lauda and Gerhard Berger won 35 Grands Prix between them, but only one of these was on home ground, when Lauda finally won at the tenth of his 11 attempts in 1984. Berger – whose career largely coincided with Austria's lack of a Grand Prix from 1988 to 1996 – is now the predominant member of this duo, having taken the helm of BMW's motorsport programme. So he will be the one to whom the Austrian fans look in the years ahead as he pushes to develop the BMW engine.

BEAUTIFUL SCENERY: The A1-Ring is blessed with a stunning mountain backdrop, but the twists and turns mean the drivers have no time to admire the view

The A1-Ring is a circuit that has a big act to follow, having been built over the Osterreichring, a circuit that was a favourite of many during its run on the Formula One World Championship calendar from 1970 to 1987; its sweeping corners bisecting the mountainside offered spectators unrivalled viewing. The Osterreichring enjoyed some classic races, such as when Elio de Angelis pipped Keke Rosberg by 0.05 seconds in 1982, and it developed a reputation for surprise results, with Vittorio Brambilla, John Watson and Alan Jones scoring their first Grand Prix wins there in consecutive years in the mid-1970s. Alas, it fell behind in terms of safety – particularly the narrowness of the pit straight, necessitating three attempts to get the 1987 race underway after start-line shunts in the first two attempts, and it was dropped from the calendar. The circuit owners redeveloped their facility in the mid-1990s and turned it into the A1-Ring. This uses the same pit area and much of the original track, but without some of its fastest sections; even the corners that were retained have been made slower. The A1-Ring was rewarded with a Grand Prix in 1997.

AN UPHILL STRUGGLE

The first thing that strikes anyone visiting the A1-Ring is how steep the climb is to the first corner. The ascent is taken at 185mph with heavy braking over a brow. It's very tight and requires drivers to grab second gear, and almost inevitably leads to contact on the first lap, as Michael Schumacher and friends discovered last year. There's then a 185mph climb through a kink to the second corner, Remus Kurve. This is approached via a sudden kick-up, and is another second-gear right-hander. It's actually an open hairpin, and has seen plenty of action, with David Coulthard's collision with team-mate Mika Hakkinen in 1999 being the most memorable.

From here, there's a gently-sloping straight – again taken at 185mph – down to the Gosser Kurve. Now a third-gear double-apex right-hander, it's on the site of the fearsome, fifth-gear Boschkurve. The track doubles back to the first of a pair of slightly-banked left-handers, Niki Lauda Kurve, followed after a downhill slope by Power Horse Kurve. Drivers then have to accelerate over a crest behind the paddock before hitting 180mph and dropping down to the penultimate corner: Jochen Rindt Kurve. It feeds straight into the final corner, the fifth-gear A1 Kurve, where so many drivers spun off or ran through the gravel in qualifying last year.

The A1-Ring may not offer the open flow of the Osterreichring, but it offers at least three potential overtaking points: under braking for the first corner; into the second; and into the third. This clearly demonstrates that the best way to provide overtaking opportunities is to have a long straight leading into a slow corner.

ROUGH AND TUMBLE

The venue's tradition of producing first-time winners almost re-emerged on the occasion of the A1-Ring's first Grand Prix in 1997, when Formula One rookie Jarno Trulli looked set for victory for Prost. Unfortunately, Williams' Jacques Villeneuve passed him during the pit-stop sequence, and then Trulli had to retire when his engine blew. The A1-Ring's second race was a McLaren one-two, despite David Coulthard being pitched into a spin on the opening lap and having to pit for a new nose before fighting his way through the field. Michael Schumacher also had to pit for a new nose after a huge airborne moment out of the Jochen Rindt Kurve, and came through to third when his team-mate Eddie Irvine slowed with "brake problems".

For the second year running, Coulthard hit trouble at the second corner on the opening lap in 1999. This time, he was the one triggering the trouble, spinning team-mate Hakkinen out of the lead. Then he was outraced in the middle stages by Irvine, who took a later pit stop and emerged in a lead he was to keep, demonstrating that Ferrari could win without Michael Schumacher (who was convalescing at home after his British Grand Prix accident). Hakkinen fought through from last to third. Michael Schumacher failed to survive the first-corner traffic jam last year, and the McLarens raced off to an easy one-two, with Hakkinen re-emerging as the team's faster driver after a spell in the doldrums. Barrichello was the best of the rest for Ferrari.

UP HILL, DOWN DALE: Michael Schumacher accelerates along the top section of the A1-Ring circuit

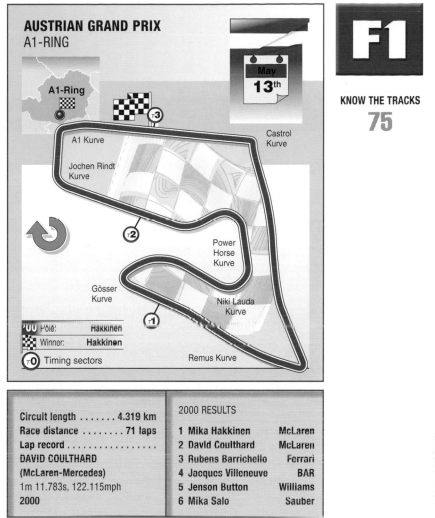

AUSTRIAN GRAND PRIX
A1-RING

May 13th

A1 Kurve
Jochen Rindt Kurve
Castrol Kurve
Power Horse Kurve
Gösser Kurve
Niki Lauda Kurve
Remus Kurve

Pole: Hakkinen
Winner: Hakkinen
Timing sectors

		2000 RESULTS	
Circuit length	4.319 km	1 Mika Hakkinen	McLaren
Race distance	71 laps	2 David Coulthard	McLaren
Lap record		3 Rubens Barrichello	Ferrari
DAVID COULTHARD		4 Jacques Villeneuve	BAR
(McLaren-Mercedes)		5 Jenson Button	Williams
1m 11.783s, 122.115mph		6 Mika Salo	Sauber
2000			

MONACO

ROUND 7: MAY 27, 2001

Monaco may not be blessed with the high-speed sweepers of the great circuits, but it remains a test of the drivers' precision, as the corners arrive every few seconds so one slip can spell disaster. Beloved of the sponsors, it's also a race that the drivers really want to win.

HERO OF THE TRACK

Ayrton Senna was a hero wherever he raced, but his tally of six wins at Monaco in seven years between 1987 and 1993 marks him out as the greatest Monaco specialist of all time. Indeed, he was also leading in the one year that broke this run, 1988, only to slide off and clip a barrier at Portier, putting him out of the race. Precision was his trademark and nowhere is it needed more than Monaco.

A driver on a quick lap around Monaco will hit 175mph after exiting the tunnel and then have to stand hard on the brakes. This will feel fast in the narrow confines of this street circuit. But it's nothing when you consider that the drivers reach 220mph at Hockenheim. Small wonder, then, that three-times World Champion Nelson Piquet described driving a Formula One car around Monaco as like riding a bicycle around your sitting room: great fun, but an accident waiting to happen. Twisty, steep and narrow, a fast lap around Monaco requires 100% concentration, or it can easily end in disaster against the barriers that surround its every metre.

NO TIME TO RELAX

Even the start/finish straight offers a challenge, as it's not straight, curving right towards Ste Devote. This right-hander is tight when taken one at a time, but it's a nightmare bottleneck on the opening lap when drivers try to take it two or three abreast. Unsurprisingly, it has seen many an accident, with the cars at the back often coming to a standstill until those ahead have untangled themselves. Even if they make it through Ste Devote, the corner can catch out the unwary. Indeed, six cars came to grief there during last year's race.

Then it's uphill to Massanet, hitting 160mph by the crest. This left-hander into Casino Square is taken blind and a driver immediately has to set up the car for the right-hander that runs out of the far side and down to the Mirabeau hairpin. The downhill Grand Hotel (formerly Loews) hairpin is next. It's not an overtaking place, but every year people try...

After the double-right onto the seafront at Portier comes the tunnel: a long right-hand arc taken at 150mph. Blinking into the daylight, drivers brake hard and jink through

PLACE YOUR BETS: Casino Square provides a famous set of twists for the drivers to negotiate

win. Two years later rain hit and young guns Ayrton Senna and Stefan Bellof were hauling in Alain Prost before the flag was brought out early. But perhaps the most gung-ho drive came from Nigel Mansell in 1992 when he threw everything at the McLaren as he tried to push his Williams back ahead after an enforced pit stop.

The 1997 encounter was also dramatic, as rain swept in and many teams found themselves on the wrong tyres. As expected, Michael Schumacher dominated for Ferrari for his third Monaco scalp in four years, backed up by Rubens Barrichello scoring a surprise second for Stewart. McLaren returned to the top in 1998 when Mika Hakkinen was able to win as he pleased once David Coulthard had retired from his tail, with Giancarlo Fisichella surviving a spin to bring his Benetton home second ahead of Eddie Irvine's Ferrari. A moment that stood out was when Schumacher barged past Alexander Wurz's Benetton at Loews, only for Wurz to repass him at the next corner.

Schumacher was the class of the field in 1999, passing Hakkinen on the run to the first corner, with Irvine demoting Coulthard to fourth. Hakkinen later slid into the escape road at Mirabeau and so fell to third. Last year's race looked to be going to Schumacher as he rocketed clear, with Jarno Trulli holding second in his Jordan and clearly delaying Coulthard. But Trulli's gearbox jammed and Coulthard was unleashed. His chase looked futile, but it paid off when Schumacher's rear suspension collapsed. Heinz-Harald Frentzen lost second when he crashed at Ste Devote, letting Ferrari's Rubens Barrichello through.

URBAN JUNGLE: It's hard to pick out there's a racing circuit at Portiers just before the track enters the tunnel

the chicane. Accelerating along the harbourside, drivers take the fast left at Tabac and then the now considerably more open left, right, right, left sequence of corners around Piscine then jink into the La Rascasse hairpin, before getting the power down up the hill through the fiddly Anthony Noghes right-hander onto the start/finish straight to complete the lap.

ONE FOR THE SPONSORS

The drivers either enjoy or loathe Monaco, with its pits and paddock crowded to bursting, their every move under intense scrutiny all weekend. Ask the sponsors, though, and they adore the race, as nowhere else on the calendar comes close for networking, with its yachts, casino and "beautiful people".

While many Grands Prix here have been processional because overtaking is so tricky, due to the narrowness of the track, there have been some fantastic ones. There was drama right to the end in 1970 when Jack Brabham locked his brakes and hit the barriers at the final corner and Jochen Rindt nipped past to win. Three drivers held the lead in the final three laps in 1982 in a race that seemingly no-one wanted to win before Riccardo Patrese recovered from a spin to

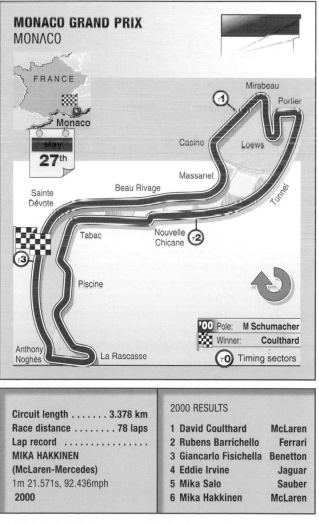

MONACO GRAND PRIX
MONACO

FRANCE

Monaco

May **27th**

Mirabeau
Portier
Casino
Loews
Massanet
Beau Rivage
Sainte Dévote
Tunnel
Nouvelle Chicane
Tabac
Piscine
Anthony Noghès
La Rascasse

'00 Pole: M Schumacher
Winner: **Coulthard**
T0 Timing sectors

Circuit length	3.378 km
Race distance	78 laps
Lap record	

MIKA HAKKINEN
(McLaren-Mercedes)
1m 21.571s, 92.436mph
2000

2000 RESULTS

1	David Coulthard	McLaren
2	Rubens Barrichello	Ferrari
3	Giancarlo Fisichella	Benetton
4	Eddie Irvine	Jaguar
5	Mika Salo	Sauber
6	Mika Hakkinen	McLaren

MONTREAL

ROUND 8: JUNE 10, 2001

The Circuit Gilles Villeneuve in Montreal is part of Formula One's furniture, a welcome mid-season expedition away from Europe to a different environment. And it never fails to entertain, or to break the cars.

HERO OF THE TRACK

Very few drivers get to race on circuits named after their father, but Jacques Villeneuve does in every Canadian GP. The Québecois fans would go wild if he were to win, but it has yet to happen in five attempts. Jacques' best result was second on the tail of team-mate Damon Hill on his first appearance in 1996, but he crashed out on the second lap in 1997 and hasn't had a competitive car since. When he does, though...

PLAYING TO THE CROWD: The tight hairpin offers an excellent chance to watch the drivers' technique in a slow corner, as well as some overtaking...

Canada has held a Grand Prix since 1967, but it wasn't until Gilles Villeneuve came along a decade later that the country's Formula One fans had anything to shout about. Indeed, only one other Canadian driver, his son Jacques, has added to the nation's victory role, but the Canadian Grand Prix is here to stay. And a very popular race it is too with all the Formula One folk.

Gilles Villeneuve pushed Formula One to heights of popularity it had never known in Canada, drawing ever more of the populace away from ice hockey and snowmobile racing. Canada suffered a huge blow when he died at Zolder in qualifying for the 1982 Belgian Grand Prix, and Canada's new-found race fans looked more to Indycar racing. Formula One only became big business again in Canada when Jacques moved across after winning the Indycar crown in 1995. With a strong chance of winning on his home debut in 1996, it seemed that everyone in Quebec wanted to see him win on the circuit named after his father, but he had to settle for second behind team-mate Damon Hill.

Canada's early Grands Prix were held on road circuits up-country at Mosport Park in Ontario and Quebec's Mont Tremblant. These races were held in the autumn, and the turning leaves on the trees that surrounded both circuits made the backdrop one of the most attractive in Formula One. With these circuits lacking in facilities, the race was then moved to its current Montreal venue, with Gilles fittingly winning the first race there in 1978.

STRAIGHTS AND ESSES

Built on the site of the EXPO 67 display, the circuit is on a long island in the St Lawrence River, with water at almost every turn, as the track runs around a boating lake and the pits back onto the rowing lake used in the 1976 Olympics.

The sprint from the grid to the first corner always sees excited jockeying for position as the track jinks right, goes tight left and then into a right-hand hairpin, the Virage Senna. And inevitably someone will get this wrong as the drivers attempt to funnel their cars into an ever-narrowing area and end up in the gravel trap there. From there, drivers must negotiate a series of esses and chicanes before touching 180mph on the curving back straight, with concrete barriers surrounding their every move. After yet another ess, comes the Casino Hairpin, the circuit's best overtaking spot. This is where Nigel Mansell waved to the fans on the final lap in 1991, only to stall and let Nelson Piquet through to win...The blast back to the pit straight is taken in sixth gear, hitting 190mph before the final chicane where so many robust overtaking manoeuvres have been executed. Watch out for the exit, as the wall there has proved "magnetic" in recent years, claiming four cars in 1999. This wall aside, expect to see retirements aplenty, as the circuit's bumps and tight corners stress the cars' moving parts like nowhere else.

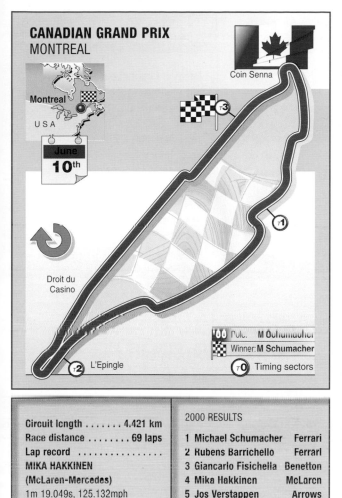

CANADIAN GRAND PRIX
MONTREAL

Montreal
USA

June
10th

Coin Senna

Droit du
Casino

L'Epingle

Pole: M Schumacher
Winner: **M Schumacher**
Timing sectors

Circuit length . . . . 4.421 km	2000 RESULTS
Race distance . . . . 69 laps	
Lap record	1 Michael Schumacher Ferrari
MIKA HAKKINEN	2 Rubens Barrichello Ferrari
(McLaren-Mercedes)	3 Giancarlo Fisichella Benetton
1m 19.049s, 125.132mph	4 Mika Hakkinen McLaren
2000	5 Jos Verstappen Arrows
	6 Jarno Trulli Jordan

HIGHS AND LOWS

The circuit's darkest day came in 1982 when Riccardo Paletti was killed when his Osella ploughed into Didier Pironi's stalled Ferrari on the grid. Since then, the worst moment came in 1997 when Olivier Panis's Prost hit the barriers at 150mph, breaking both his legs. The circuit has provided brighter moments, though, when Michael Schumacher's Benetton faltered and Jean Alesi scored his one and only victory here in 1995, to the delight of not just his Ferrari team but everyone in the paddock.

Recent races have been dramatic, as in 1998 when Alexander Wurz was launched over Alesi's Sauber, his Benetton cart-wheeling into the gravel trap where it was joined by the entire midfield and necessitated a restart. With the McLarens both hitting mechanical troubles, Michael Schumacher then dominated for Ferrari, but he was fortunate to escape censure for pitching Heinz-Harald Frentzen's Williams off the track as he left the pits. Hakkinen pressurized Schumacher into making a mistake in 1999 and took over at the front to win as he pleased, with Frentzen crashing out of second with four laps to go, handing the place to Benetton's Giancarlo Fisichella.

However, it was Ferrari all the way last year as Michael Schumacher controlled proceedings once McLaren's David Coulthard was called in from second for a stop-go penalty earned when his mechanics attended to his car on the grid after they should have withdrawn. Barrichello closed onto Schumacher's tail in the wet closing laps, having lost time with an extra stop after the team wrongly predicted the weather.

WATCH OUT!: The concrete walls line the entire length of the circuit, with this wall at the beginning of the start/ finish straight proving an almost magnetic attraction to the drivers

ROUND 9: JUNE 24, 2001

The Nurburgring was maligned when it was recreated in the mid-1980s as a shadow of its old self, but its twisting format seldom fails to provide an interesting race, especially when the regular rain sweeps in mid-race.

A GOLDEN SHADOW: Jacques Villeneuve races to victory through the Castrol-S in 1997

WATCH OUT FOR THE FIRST CORNER

The Nurburgring's first corner never fails to entertain. It's a right-hander approached in sixth at around 185mph, and drivers need to scrub off 100mph and drop three gears to negotiate it. Many fail, especially on the first lap as they funnel their cars onto a very narrow racing line, and several invariably end up in the huge gravel trap, out of which some emerge providing they've managed not to become bogged down.

The first corner is followed immediately by a left-hander, after which many of those who messed up the first corner often rejoin. Then it's downhill through a left, a tighter right and a second-gear, right-hand hairpin at the lowest point of the circuit. Then it's uphill, with flat-out acceleration to a left-right ess and then the RTL Kurve, a tricky left that caught out Damon Hill in 1995. The track dips through the right-hand Bitkurve, then it's a flat-out blast through a sixth-gear kink and on up an incline to the tight Veedol-S chicane where drivers take any number of lines both around and sometimes over the kerbs. Good speed out of here is vital, as is a clean exit from the final hairpin to get into position to slingshot past the car ahead into the first corner.

A VERY DIFFERENT FOREBEAR

Glance at the Nurburgring's history dating back to 1927 and it's very clear that the circuit used today is not to be confused with the one that hosted Germany's annual showpiece event from 1951 to 1976. That

British race fans have every reason to be jealous of their German counterparts. For not only do they have the unfailingly competitive Michael Schumacher to cheer on, but they are treated to two "home" Grands Prix per year. One is the German GP at Hockenheim. However, largely since Schumacher became a regular winner in the mid-1990s, they've had a second race within their borders at the Nurburgring, called the European GP or occasionally the Luxembourg GP. With Heinz-Harald Frentzen, Michael's brother Ralf and Nick Heidfeld to support, along with engine suppliers BMW and Mercedes, Germany is a major player in Formula One. However, Britain also had four drivers of the 22 in last year's top rank, to say nothing of being home to seven of the 11 teams. So there's a good case for the title of the European GP to be used occasionally for a second race in Britain.

LEADEN SKIES: The Nürburgring's location in the Eifel mountains means that the weather is usually changeable, between cold and wet...

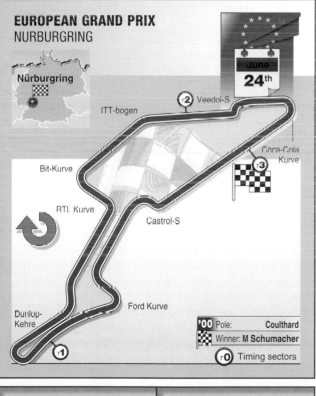

EUROPEAN GRAND PRIX
NURBURGRING

Nürburgring

JUNE
24th

Veedol-S

ITT-bogen

Coca-Cola
Kurve

Bit-Kurve

RTL Kurve

Castrol-S

Ford Kurve

Dunlop-
Kehre

'00 Pole: Coulthard
Winner: M Schumacher
Timing sectors

Circuit length . . . . 4.556 km	
Race distance . . . . 67 laps	
Lap record	
HEINZ-HARALD FRENTZEN	
(Williams-Renault)	
1m 18.805s, 129.330mph	
1997	

2000 RESULTS

1	Michael Schumacher	Ferrari
2	Mika Hakkinen	McLaren
3	David Coulthard	McLaren
4	Rubens Barrichello	Ferrari
5	Giancarlo Fisichella	Benetton
6	Pedro de la Rosa	Arrows

was known as the Nordschleife circuit, and was 14 miles long with corners almost too numerous to count at over 100 in number and certainly too numerous to remember well. Outdated by the mid-1970s, the drivers were making noises about it being too dangerous for Formula One use when Niki Lauda was nearly killed there in 1976. The Grand Prix was moved to Hockenheim with immediate effect.

The Nurburgring we know today shares little more than the name, the location and the frequently wet weather with its predecessor. It was built around the pits area of the old track, and instead of a narrow track winding through the trees, with blind brows and steeply banked corners, it's wide, open and surrounded by gravel traps. With the grandstands set well back from the track, the immediacy of its predecessor is lost. Indeed, spectators living in the Nordschleife were able to watch cars race past just three or four metres from them. Despite initial criticism, it's not such a bad circuit. And it has staged some excellent races since 1984's European GP. The 1995 race was a real highlight as Michael Schumacher chased Jean Alesi's Ferrari and then took the lead with just two laps left, to all but clinch his second world title for Benetton.

The first corner looms large as the venue for much of the action over the years, as Schumacher was knocked out of the race there by his brother Ralf in 1997 and the McLarens both blew up within a lap of each other when racing clear, handing a soft win to Jacques Villeneuve. Michael Schumacher was on pole in 1998, but he was overhauled by Hakkinen who stayed out for a longer first stint. Rain didn't spoil play in 1999: it improved it, and the order was truly shuffled as Heinz-Harald Frentzen led for Jordan then retired, letting David Coulthard take over. But he crashed out. So too did Giancarlo Fisichella, leaving the way clear for Johnny Herbert to guess the changeable weather best to give Stewart its only Grand Prix win. Last year, Michael Schumacher overhauled Hakkinen's McLaren and proved his superiority in wet conditions by pulling clear when it started to rain.

ROUND 10: JULY 1, 2001

It will come as quite a shock to its critics, but Magny-Cours provides some of the best racing of the Formula One World Championship, as anyone who recalls last year's race will confirm.

France has a special place in motorsport history in that it hosted the first ever race back in 1894, along public roads between Paris and Rouen. With marques such as Bugatti, Delage, Talbot and Gordini to the fore, France was a major player until the Second World War, after which the Italians took over, then the Germans and then the British in the 1960s. France still hosts one of the world's most prestigious races in the shape of the annual Le Mans 24 Hours sportscar race, but in Formula One terms it is losing touch – as the form of its one team, Prost, demonstrated last year.

A RACE ON THE MOVE

The French Grand Prix has moved around a lot over the years: six circuits hosted the race before it moved to Magny-Cours in 1991.

Deprived of the Grand Prix, these other circuits have fallen a long way behind in terms of facilities and investment, with only Paul Ricard thought capable of regaining the race.

Reims was the first French venue to hold a modern-day (post-1950) Grand Prix on an almost triangular course of public roads, with its races famed for drivers hunting in packs as they used each other's slipstreams to haul themselves up to the cars ahead. Interspersed in the same period from the early 1950s to the late 1960s, the Rouen-les-Essarts track was used, complete with a cobbled hairpin... Perhaps France's greatest track was used next, high on the hill above Clermont-Ferrand. Twisting through fast and often blind corners, it was a classic, but it was judged too dangerous as the cars became faster. Thus the flat Paul Ricard circuit just behind the Riviera took

over in 1971, with the Grand Prix staying there with occasional forays to the hillier Dijon-Prenois circuit before Magny-Cours began its reign.

In the days when Paul Ricard and Dijon-Prenois shared the Grand Prix, Magny-Cours was a club circuit. But it had the good fortune to be located in a backward rural area. President Mitterand decided it should be transformed into a centre of technical excellence to help bring wealth to the region.

WATCH FOR THE HAIRPIN

Despite its lack of popularity, Magny-Cours offers the drivers quite a challenge. The best of the lap comes at the start, with the tightening 165mph Grande Courbe left-hander feeding downhill into the long Estoril right-

ROOMS WITH A VIEW: The hospitality suites look right down onto the grid. This is Schumacher on pole last year

A TIGHT RIGHT: Michael Schumacher leads the McLarens of David Coulthard and Mika Hakkinen plus his own team-mate Rubens Barrichello through Chateau d'Eau and down towards the pits

hander that spits the cars back out onto the long climb to the chief overtaking point on the whole track: the Adelaide hairpin. Right at the top of the hill, drivers have to drop from 180mph to 35mph as they turn right, often having to choose between slow in and fast out and going in wide, or taking a tight line according to whether they are attacking or defending. After this, the track twists down through the Nurburgring ess to 180. Fittingly, this corner turns the track through 180 degrees, pointing it back uphill through the undulating Imola ess into the Chateau d'Eau right-hander and the drop down to the track's tightest chicane before the final corner, the tight Lycée right-hander onto the pit straight.

A German clean sweep of the front of the grid was notable in 1997, with Michael Schumacher taking pole ahead of Heinz-Harald Frentzen and brother Ralf. And while Ralf fell to sixth, Michael led Heinz-Harald home in a race that was brought to life by rain in the closing laps. When the 1998 race had to be restarted, Michael Schumacher got the jump on Mika Hakkinen to lead away. With team-mate Irvine slotting into second place, he was able to escape as the McLaren drivers were delayed. Hakkinen eventually passed Irvine, only to spin, while David Coulthard hit refuelling problems and had to make two extra pit stops.

Rain was the making of the race in 1999. Indeed, five drivers had a turn in the lead. Coulthard retired when pulling clear and left Barrichello back in the lead for Stewart. Hakkinen then spun trying to pass him and had to fight his way back to the front, which he did. But the win went to Heinz-Harald Frentzen who'd had his Jordan filled with sufficient fuel to complete the race when everyone pitted for rain tyres.

Coulthard gained revenge last year when he was in feisty form as he fought his way past both Ferrari drivers – letting Schumacher know what he thought of his driving as he battled his way past. Schumacher then retired from second place when his engine blew, promoting Hakkinen.

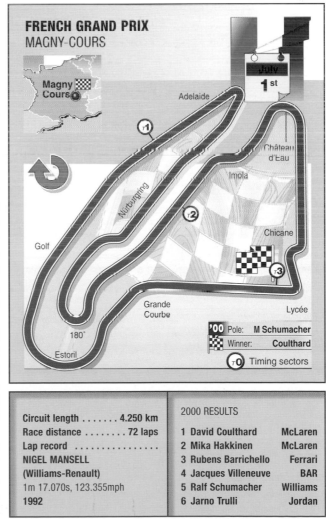

FRENCH GRAND PRIX
MAGNY-COURS

Magny Cours

July
1st

Adelaide

Château d'Eau

Imola

Nurburgring

Chicane

Golf

Grande Courbe

Lycée

180°

Estoril

'00 Pole: M Schumacher
Winner: Coulthard
70 Timing sectors

Circuit length . . . . 4.250 km	
Race distance . . . . 72 laps	
Lap record	
NIGEL MANSELL	
(Williams-Renault)	
1m 17.070s, 123.355mph	
1992	

2000 RESULTS

1	David Coulthard	McLaren
2	Mika Hakkinen	McLaren
3	Rubens Barrichello	Ferrari
4	Jacques Villeneuve	BAR
5	Ralf Schumacher	Williams
6	Jarno Trulli	Jordan

SILVERSTONE

ROUND 11: JULY 15, 2001

Silverstone used to have a vice-like grip on hosting the British Grand Prix, but last year it resisted a challenge by Brands Hatch and was then delighted to be granted the Grand Prix for a further 15 years.

READY, STEADY, GO: Rubens Barrichello and Heinz-Harald Frentzen wait for the fifth red light to go on and then go out again

E ven though the British GP has been moved back to July after a swap with the Austrian GP, everyone will be praying for dry weather before this year's race so that there is no repeat of last year's scenes of cars stuck in quagmires in the car parks. Many said that this was a case of Silverstone not getting its act together last year, but matters probably weren't helped by the race moving from July to the end of April – the wettest April in more than a century as it happened. In an attempt to ease traffic jams, the organizers are restricting car parking to encourage fans to go by coach, as they can ill afford more censure from the FIA.

Silverstone has a special place in history as the venue for the first round of the inaugural World Championship in 1950. Only two years old then, Silverstone has been transformed ever since, although its nature remains the same as a high-speed circuit around an airfield. British teams had struggled when the British GP was held at Donington Park before the Second World War when Alfa Romeo and Auto Union dominated. Alfa Romeo was back in control when Silverstone became the race's new venue, and the first British win didn't come until 1955. This wasn't in a British car, but a

Mercedes, and not at Silverstone but at Aintree, the home of the Grand National horse race where Stirling Moss pipped team-mate Juan Manuel Fangio on a track that ran around the perimeter.

Two years later, Moss won in a British Vanwall that he shared with compatriot Tony Brooks. The race alternated between Aintree and Silverstone until 1962. Then Brands Hatch took over the alternate slot in 1964. However, Brands Hatch lost the battle to host the race after 1986, and only now is it undertaking the safety work required before it can regain the race.

FLAT IN PARTS

Silverstone's Copse Corner is one of the fastest opening corners, being taken at 140mph in fourth gear before the drivers hit 180mph as they jink through Maggotts into the Becketts esses. This is taken at 115mph as it dives right, flicks left and then right. Then it's flat-out through Chapel and onto the Hangar Straight and up to 195mph before braking hard down to 105mph at Stowe so the driver can turn in to the Vale dip. Hard left and uphill at the end of this, it's right through Club and up to 170mph before the chicane at Abbey. This used to be the fastest corner, but it now slows the cars so that they don't arrive so fast at Bridge. This is still daunting as the cars dive into a dip at 155mph and then turn hard right, firing up into the 'infield section'. This section offers great viewing as it twists in front of the grandstands. A left at Priory, another at Brooklands, then a right through Luffield and another at Woodcote complete the lap.

THE GREAT RACES

One of the greatest races ever held at Silverstone was in 1987, and it's one that's remembered for its duel between Nigel Mansell and his Williams team-mate Nelson Piquet. They ran wheel-to-wheel down the Hangar Straight before the crowd went mad when the local hero passed the Brazilian into Stowe. There was also a great scrap between Damon Hill and Williams team leader Alain Prost in 1993. Just when it looked as though Hill was set to score his first win, however, his engine blew.

The 1998 race will rank as one of the most confusing, with rain bringing out the safety car as cars aquaplaned, wiping out Hakkinen's 30-second lead. It ended in confusion when new leader Michael Schumacher was penalized for passing under waved yellows, and chose to call in for his stop-go penalty after the finish. Amazingly, he was allowed to keep his win... David Coulthard took the trophy in 1999 in a race in which Schumacher crashed at Stowe after the red flags came out on the first lap, breaking a leg. Hakkinen had wheel problems in the pits when leading the restarted race, and then had his right rear wheel partly fall off, by which time Coulthard was through and clear.

Last year's race saw Silverstone waterlogged, but the race itself went ahead in dry weather. Barrichello led away from Heinz-Harald Frentzen. Coulthard got the jump on Hakkinen for third. Schumacher tried to pass too, but skidded on the grass and fell from fifth to eighth. Frentzen was running a two-stop strategy so fell behind the McLarens. Coulthard saw his chance when Barrichello's Ferrari stuttered, taking the lead into Stowe. Three laps later, Barrichello was out. Coulthard was slowed with gearshift problems but held on to win from Hakkinen, with Schumacher climbing to third.

APRIL SHOWERS: Last year's British Grand Prix suffered from flooded carparks after yet more rain

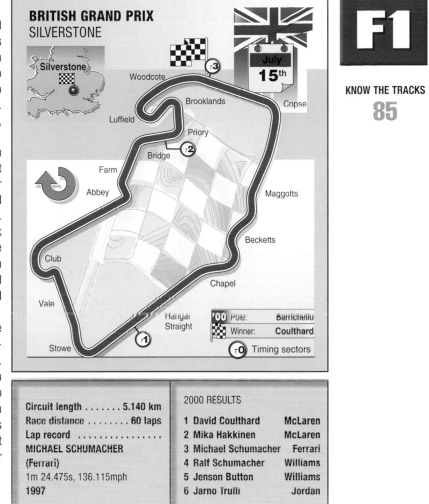

BRITISH GRAND PRIX
SILVERSTONE

Silverstone

July **15th**

Woodcote — Brooklands — Copse — Luffield — Priory — Bridge — Farm — Abbey — Maggotts — Club — Becketts — Chapel — Vale — Hangar Straight — Stowe

Pole: Barrichello
Winner: Coulthard
Timing sectors

	2000 RESULTS	
Circuit length . . . . 5.140 km		
Race distance . . . . 60 laps	1 David Coulthard	McLaren
Lap record	2 Mika Hakkinen	McLaren
MICHAEL SCHUMACHER	3 Michael Schumacher	Ferrari
(Ferrari)	4 Ralf Schumacher	Williams
1m 24.475s, 136.115mph	5 Jenson Button	Williams
1997	6 Jarno Trulli	Jordan

F1 HOCKENHEIM

ROUND 12: JULY 29, 2001

Hockenheim earned infamy last year when a spectator ran onto the track. Otherwise, the circuit conjures up images of 215mph straights, chicanes and a twisty stadium section surrounded by massive grandstands. This year, let's hope that it's remembered for racing.

HERO OF THE TRACK

It's not often that someone who is a local hero has never raced in Formula One, but Willi Weber is such a man. However, it's for the fact that he discovered Michael Schumacher and propelled him to Formula One and then did the same with Ralf that he is lauded by the hundreds of thousands of flag-waving Germans who pack Hockenheim's huge grandstands and surrounding forests. Without Willi's intervention, Germany would probably still be awaiting its first World Champion.

THROUGH THE FOREST: The cars blast flat-out through the forest, hitting 215mph before braking to 70mph for the three chicanes that break its flow. This is the approach to the Ostkurve

Think German Grand Prix and you tend to think of Hockenheim, although the race hasn't always been held there. Indeed, with only two exceptions, it was held at the Nurburgring from 1951 to 1976, and only handed over to Hockenheim after Niki Lauda nearly met his death at the 'Ring in 1976.

The Nurburgring was famed for being 14 miles long, offering more than 100 corners, with points where the cars get airborne and others where drivers would have to fight to keep away from the trees. Already concerned by its dangers, Lauda voiced his fears before the Grand Prix in 1976 and then very nearly proved himself right....

The Grand Prix was held at the Avus circuit in Berlin in 1959, where two banked corners were joined by enormously long straights. And the other occasion on which the Nurburgring was left silent was in 1970 when the race moved to Hockenheim, a circuit that had claimed the life of World

Champion Jim Clark in a Formula Two race in 1968.

In 1977, the Grand Prix came to Hockenheim for good, but it took years to become liked by the sport's insiders, even though there have been some great races with slipstreaming packs jousting their way down the flat-out straights. The grandstands have been packed every year since, with the exception of 1985 when the race returned to the Nurburgring – not to the original Nordschleife version of the Nurburgring, but to a modern circuit built around the old pits.

TWO CIRCUITS IN ONE

Hockenheim is a Jekyll and Hyde sort of circuit, with one part tight and twisty, the other flat-out straights and chicanes. The first corner, the Nordkurve, is a fourth-gear right-hander, where Michael Schumacher and Giancarlo Fisichella clashed last year. Then it's a 215mph blast to the first chicane, the Jim Clark Kurve. Ability on the brakes is a must as cars need to drop to 60mph for the second-gear right-left before it's flat-out again to the far end of the loop and the Ostkurve chicane. A third straight bends right before straightening to the third chicane. Known as the Ayrton Senna Kurve, this differs in that it's left then right, although cars occasionally run straight on with spectacular results, such as when Pedro Diniz hit Jean Alesi last year. A final straight leads them into the stadium section at the Agip Kurve right-hander. This is followed by the Sachs Kurve, a second-gear left-hander,

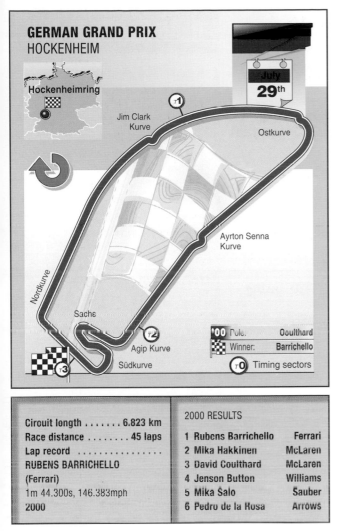

GERMAN GRAND PRIX
HOCKENHEIM

Hockenheimring

July
29th

Jim Clark Kurve

Ostkurve

Ayrton Senna Kurve

Nordkurve

Sachs

Agip Kurve

Südkurve

'00 Pole: Coulthard
Winner: Barrichello

0 Timing sectors

Circuit length . . . . 6.823 km	
Race distance . . . . 45 laps	
Lap record	
RUBENS BARRICHELLO	
(Ferrari)	
1m 44.300s, 146.383mph	
2000	

2000 RESULTS

1	Rubens Barrichello	Ferrari
2	Mika Hakkinen	McLaren
3	David Coulthard	McLaren
4	Jenson Button	Williams
5	Mika Salo	Sauber
6	Pedro de la Rosa	Arrows

TOTAL CONTRAST: After the blast through the silence of the forest, the drivers burst into a wall of sound from the spectators as they turn right through Agip Kurve into the stadium section. This is the slightly-banked Sachs Kurve that feeds the track around the back of the paddock

before the lap is completed by a kink, then the double-apex Sudkurve right-hander.

Plans were mooted for the "country section" to be curtailed so that the lap length was cut from 6.8km to 4.5km by lopping off the Ostkurve, but environmental protests have delayed planning permission and so the earliest that a reduced Hockenheim will appear is 2002.

THE NOISIEST CROWD

Any circuit is a Michael Schumacher sort of circuit, but few grandstands are as full of Schumacher and Ferrari banners as those that surround Hockenheim's 150,000-seater stadium section. The noise they make with their air horns whenever he appears is outrageous and must be worth a fraction of a second per lap for the boost that it gives him. You certainly can't miss his emergence from the Ferrari pit garage. Even if he is only sticking his head out in order to check on the weather.

A winner at Hockenheim in 1995, Schumacher loves the place, but it has been a far happier hunting ground for Gerhard Berger. He won here in 1994 to bring to an end Ferrari's longest run without a win. In 1996, he was poised to put Benetton back at the front after a barren spell following Schumacher's departure for Ferrari, when his engine blew. The following year, he came back from illness, his father's death and the news that he had no future with Benetton by starting on pole, setting fastest lap and winning.

Schumacher's hopes of adding to his one German GP win came to nought in 1998 when Mika Hakkinen and David Coulthard dominated in their McLarens. Schumacher finished fifth. A broken leg meant his only involvement in 1999 was to broadcast a message to his fans over the circuit's giant screens. Matters failed to improve for "Schumi" last year when he went out in a first-corner accident. The McLarens were already ahead and pulled clear for what looked sure to be a one-two until a safety-car intervention to clear a spectator from trackside. Coulthard fell from second to sixth in this sequence, then rain hit with 12 laps to go and Rubens Barrichello chose right in staying out on dry-weather tyres for his first-ever win to send Ferrari home with some consolation.

HUNGARORING

ROUND 13: AUGUST 19, 2001

Tight and twisty, the Hungaroring has been described by ITV commentator Martin Brundle as "Monaco without the buildings". Add often soaring temperatures and the circuit is a thorough work-out for both driver and machine.

Hungary has held a Grand Prix since 1986. However, only those with access to the history books will know that the eastern European country held a Grand Prix once before, back in 1936 when Tazio Nuvolari won at a circuit in Budapest's Nepliget Park in his Alfa Romeo. Then Hungary's politics changed to communism, so it came as quite a surprise when it was granted a round of the World Championship before the fall of the Iron Curtain. However, the Grand Prix has thrived, with a sell-out crowd every year attracted by the excellent spectating afforded by the Hungaroring's setting in a natural amphitheatre.

Built just a short drive to the north-east of Hungary's beautiful capital city of Budapest, the first thing that strikes you is that the Hungaroring is tight and twisty, offering few overtaking places. Indeed, with its abrasive surface and frequently sweltering temperatures, teams stop twice or even three times for new rubber, so much of the overtaking is done in the pitting sequence. There tends to be just one line around the circuit, making overtaking difficult, especially as it's notoriously slippery off-line, so drivers have to be on their toes throughout, something that isn't easy as they ward off heat exhaustion.

UP HILL AND DOWN DALE

The Hungaroring is blessed with wonderful terrain, the circuit spanning both sides of a wooded valley, offering fantastic views of much of the track. The lap starts high on one side of the valley, with the slope providing a natural grandstand along the start/finish straight. This drops towards its end into a 180-degree right-hander that dips from entry to exit as it doubles back. A short straight that is the scene of much jousting on the first lap follows, before a downhill left-hander and then a dipping right-hander that pours the drivers onto a straight dropping to the bottom

PREPARE TO QUALIFY: Pedro de la Rosa leaves the pitlane in his Arrows, with the Hungaroring's 14 corners already mapped out in his mind. Sadly, his planning counted for little worthwhile as his car wasn't competitive on last year's visit

of the valley. Cars hit 175mph here before climbing up the far side of the valley and kinking left. A right-hander leads the cars onto a flat but twisty section that starts with a chicane then jinks left, right and left until it reaches Turn Eleven and drops to the right and down to Turn Twelve. Then the track rises all the way up to the 14th and last corner, a double-apex right-hander onto the start/finish straight. If a driver wants to make the most of the circuit's best overtaking opportunity – into the first corner – he must get a good exit speed here in order to get into the slipstream of the car ahead and then pull past before they start braking from 180mph.

HILL'S HAPPY HUNTING GROUND

The first race at the all-new Hungaroring resulted in victory for Nelson Piquet in his Williams ahead of Ayrton Senna's Lotus, with the rest a lap and more behind. With 200,000 spectators turning out for this inaugural Grand Prix, Hungary had made its mark. Piquet won again in 1987, then in 1988 Senna triumphed by just half a second from his McLaren team-mate Alain Prost. Senna won again in 1991 and 1992, resisting a charge from Nigel Mansell in the second of these, but second that day after a great recovery from a puncture was enough for the English driver to clinch the World Championship in 1992.

Damon Hill has fond memories of the Hungaroring, as it was here that he scored his first Grand Prix win in 1993, winning again in 1995. He nearly won for a third time in 1997, albeit this time in an Arrows, shocking everyone as he wrung speed from the car that it had never previously displayed. With his Bridgestone tyres working better than the Goodyears on which the majority of the frontrunners were using, he qualified third then passed Michael Schumacher's Ferrari for the lead. Having pulled clear, his gearbox started to fail. Former Williams team-mate Jacques Villeneuve passed him halfway around the final lap, but he hung on to finish second.

The following year, Ross Brawn masterminded Michael Schumacher's victory over the superior McLarens by putting the German onto a three-stop strategy that counted for double. Mika Hakkinen then dominated in 1999, with team-mate David Coulthard passing Ferrari's Eddie Irvine for second. Last year's race was expected to be between pole-sitter Michael Schumacher and

A WASTED OPPORTUNITY: David Coulthard started from pole last year, but was back in third place by the first corner and remained there for the whole race

Coulthard, but Hakkinen rocketed past both from the second row of the grid and drove faultlessly to a second consecutive win as Coulthard became bottled up behind Schumacher and had to settle for third place.

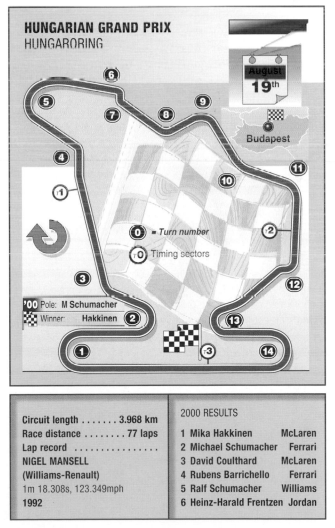

HUNGARIAN GRAND PRIX
HUNGARORING

August 19th

Budapest

0 = Turn number

Timing sectors

'00 Pole: M Schumacher
Winner: Hakkinen

Circuit length	3.968 km
Race distance	77 laps
Lap record	
NIGEL MANSELL	
(Williams-Renault)	
1m 18.308s, 123.349mph	
1992	

2000 RESULTS		
1 Mika Hakkinen	McLaren	
2 Michael Schumacher	Ferrari	
3 David Coulthard	McLaren	
4 Rubens Barrichello	Ferrari	
5 Ralf Schumacher	Williams	
6 Heinz-Harald Frentzen	Jordan	

SPA-FRANCORCHAMPS

ROUND 14: SEPTEMBER 2, 2001

A Grand Prix win at any circuit is worth 10 points, but a win at Spa-Francorchamps carries far more credence than most as it's the world's greatest racing circuit, the one that tests the driver to the full. It's simply magnificent.

HERO OF THE TRACK

For all the skills of Belgium's own Jacky Ickx, no Belgian driver has won the Belgian GP. Ayrton Senna won it four years running, but so did Jim Clark in the 1960s when the full-length original Spa-Francorchamps circuit was used. The Scot loathed the place for its danger and its propensity to claim drivers' lives, but he put these fears to one side as he used his skills to their full to make the place his own.

A SHARP RIGHT: Eddie Irvine guides his Jaguar past the famous old cafe at the La Source hairpin before plunging past the old pits towards the fearsomely daunting Eau Rouge twister

If anyone ever offers the opinion that Formula One drivers don't earn their corn, take them to Spa-Francorchamps. They won't fail to be impressed by the sheer speed with which the drivers routinely take corners of ferocious difficulty. A few minutes at Eau Rouge alone will restore the faith of the most sceptical: this is a corner where drivers have to will their throttle foot to stay down when their brain is screaming for it to lift.

The circuit is located in the Ardennes hills in eastern Belgium, in the forests on the edge of the village of Francorchamps a few miles up the hill from the town of Spa. It's blessed with challenging terrain plus a handful of the best corners in the world: Eau Rouge, Pouhon and Blanchimont.

The circuit was frighteningly fast in its original form, when it was almost twice the length and used to dive into the valley towards Malmedy before rejoining the current circuit on the hill up from Stavelot, with nothing to stop cars from taking to the trees that lined its length. To make it even more of a lottery, the region's weather is changeable, with sudden heavy showers often hitting one end of the track and not the other.

UP HILL AND DOWN DALE

The first 100 metres look simple as it's a sprint uphill past the pits to the La Source hairpin, which never looks narrower than when the field is bunched on the opening lap. The corner widens on the exit, allowing a variety of lines, before the track plunges down to Eau Rouge where it snaps into a steep ascent through a left-right ess, all taken in sixth gear. The track crests the slope at Raidillon and veers left. Not surprisingly, there have been major accidents here, including Alessandro Zanardi in his Lotus in 1993 and then Jacques Villeneuve in 1998 and 1999 as the Canadian tried to take the corner without lifting.

The reason for trying to take Eau Rouge flat is that it's followed by a long straight up to the esses at Les Combes, a favourite overtaking place for those who manage to get a tow. The track cuts away from the course of the original circuit and dips into a long downhill section that starts with the Rivage hairpin then flows through a kink and down to Pouhon, an off-camber double-apex left-hander taken at 150mph. The Fagnes sweepers take the track to its lowest point, where it rejoins the original circuit then climbs through the flat-out left at Blanchimont. The final corner – the Bus Stop chicane – breaks this uphill charge, with drivers often trying to overtake on the way in, before bouncing over the kerbs on the way out and accelerating onto the curving start/finish straight.

A MOVEABLE FEAST

The Belgian Grand Prix hasn't always been held at Spa-Francorchamps, as Belgians are either Flems from the western end of the country or French-speaking Walloons from the end of the country that contains Spa-Francorchamps, and the race has been shared between them. The race was given to the Flems in the 1970s, when it was held twice at Nivelles near Brussels and then at Zolder near Liège. After Gilles Villeneuve died at Zolder in 1982, however, the race returned to Spa-Francorchamps.

Ayrton Senna provided one of the circuit's best memories on the revived circuit by starring on slicks in the rain in 1992. But the rain worsened and Michael Schumacher raced through for his first win. Since then, Schumacher has continued to be the man to beat, especially in 1997 when he anticipated the changing weather and raced clear as it rained. He looked to have done the same again in 1998, but hit David Coulthard when the McLaren driver slowed when being lapped. This left Damon Hill clear to give Jordan its first win ahead of team-mate Ralf Schumacher.

In 1999, with McLaren refusing to make Mika Hakkinen undisputed number one so that he could be helped to the title, Coulthard didn't cede on the run to the first corner and they touched. No damage was done, and Coulthard raced on to victory with a sulky Hakkinen having to settle for second. The event was marked by both BAR drivers destroying their cars at Eau Rouge in practice.

Last year's wet/dry race was marked by a brave overtaking manoeuvre by Hakkinen as he burst out of Schumacher's slipstream as the German lapped Ricardo Zonta's BAR into Les Combes, and passed both up the inside with not an inch to spare. He then motored away, leaving a shocked Schumacher trailing in his wake.

HILL-TOP SEQUENCE: Jenson Button twists his way through the left-right at Les Combes after climbing from Eau Rouge

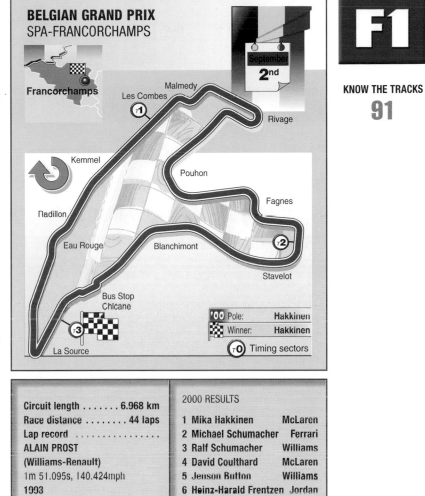

BELGIAN GRAND PRIX
SPA-FRANCORCHAMPS

September 2nd

Francorchamps

Malmedy
Les Combes
Rivage
Kemmel
Pouhon
Fagnes
Radillon
Eau Rouge
Blanchimont
Stavelot
Bus Stop Chicane
La Source

'00 Pole: Hakkinen
Winner: Hakkinen
Timing sectors

Circuit length . . . . 6.968 km	2000 RESULTS	
Race distance . . . . 44 laps	1 Mika Hakkinen	McLaren
Lap record	2 Michael Schumacher	Ferrari
ALAIN PROST	3 Ralf Schumacher	Williams
(Williams-Renault)	4 David Coulthard	McLaren
1m 51.095s, 140.424mph	5 Jenson Button	Williams
1993	6 Heinz-Harald Frentzen	Jordan

MONZA

ROUND 15: SEPTEMBER 16, 2001

Few circuits are packed with such one-eyed fans as Monza, with the *tifosi* wanting a Ferrari win, regardless of who is driving. For all that, the home of the Italian Grand Prix offers exciting racing and a wonderful atmosphere.

If you want to be part of the in-crowd at the Italian Grand Prix, wear red. For Monza is in Ferrari country. Not just because Ferrari has won the Italian Grand Prix more times than any other team, but because every Italian fan believes that their blood is red due only to team allegiance. It matters not whether the driver at the wheel of the winning car is Italian, as proved when Michael Schumacher won here last year, just that the car is a Ferrari.

Along with this patriotic support, Monza is also imbued with a glorious history that dates all the way back to 1922 when the circuit in the royal park to the north of Milan hosted the Italian Grand Prix for the first time. The circuit has changed many times in the intervening years, with the most famous feature to have been shaved from the layout being the banked corners that were last used by the Formula One cars back in 1961. Yet visit it today, and those banked corners

are still there, a decaying but wonderful reminder of what heroes those racers of old were. Walk past the pits towards the first chicane and you will spot the banking, this part of one of the 180-degree bends at either end of an oval that was part of the original layout, linked to the road course that is still used today. Safety requirements have chopped and changed the circuit from how it was, but Monza remains a wonderful place for Grand Prix racing.

HERO OF THE TRACK

Peter Gethin won just one Grand Prix, but is a hero of Monza as he came out on top in the tightest finish in Formula One history here in 1971. There were no chicanes then and slipstreaming was everything down the straights, with Peter bringing his BRM onto the tail of the leading bunch and then bursting through on the run from the final corner to pip Ronnie Peterson by 0.01 second, with the first five cars covered by just 0.61 seconds...

OVERFLOWING PASSION: Thank goodness there are no support races held after the Grand Prix, as the *tifosi* pour out onto the track every year

FLAT-OUT ALMOST EVERYWHERE

The first chicane was modified for last year's race so that it turned sharp right and then left rather than the less extreme left-right-left-right chicane of old where so many cars speared over the kerbs and into the cars ahead. Despite this enforced break in the circuit's natural flow, Formula One cars still take the following Curva Grande in fifth gear at around 175mph.

This is followed by a straight to the two Lesmo corners broken by the Curva della Roggia chicane, which was also revised last year. Even with this speed reduction, the Lesmo right-handers are a challenge. Then the cars accelerate down a straight under the old banked circuit into the Variante Ascari chicane where there used to be a wicked left-hander. Cars top 200mph on the straight to the 180-degree final corner, the Parabolica, out of which the cars are fired onto the start/finish straight.

A BROKEN FLOW

The key ingredient in success at Monza over the years has been the ability to run fast down the lengthy straights, as shown by Peter Gethin's victory in 1971 when his BRM burst from a five-car slipstreaming pack to win at an average speed of 150.755mph, a record that stands to this day as the fastest Grand Prix of all time.

It was thought that slipstreaming packs would be a thing of the past after chicanes were inserted, but there was a pack hunting for victory again in 1997, running nose-to-tail before David Coulthard

A VIEW FROM ABOVE: The impressive length and width of the start/finish straight is shown by the diminutive size of the grid in this photograph taken from the first chicane looking back towards the exit of the Parabolica

won for McLaren by a short nose from Jean Alesi's Benetton and Heinz-Harald Frentzen's Williams. But this was a very different race thanks to the track's current shape. And the Scot only moved from third to first thanks to a slick pit stop. Of overtaking on the track, there was sadly very little.

Schumacher and Eddie Irvine finishing in first and second places for Ferrari in 1998 put Schumacher level on points with McLaren's Mika Hakkinen with two races to go and moved Ferrari to within 10 points of McLaren in the Constructors' Championship. By all rights, that race should have belonged to Coulthard, but his engine blew when he was leading and Schumacher passed Hakkinen for the lead on the same lap when they were unsighted by smoke from Shinji Nakano's blown engine. Hakkinen then spun and limped despondently to the finish in fourth place as Irvine and Ralf Schumacher demoted him.

Hakkinen then threw away victory in 1999 when he inexplicably crashed out at the first chicane when running clear in the lead, handing victory to Jordan's Heinz-Harald Frentzen ahead of Ralf Schumacher's Williams and Ferrari stand-in Mika Salo. The sight of Hakkinen sobbing at the trackside showed how much winning would have meant to him.

Last year's race was the most dramatic for years. Insiders had feared that the revised first chicane would be the scene of a pile-up on the opening lap. Instead, it was the modified second chicane that caused the problem, with Frentzen triggering an accident that eliminated six cars, and a marshal was tragically killed by flying debris. Michael Schumacher was ahead of the incident and raced to his third win at Monza in five years, with Hakkinen having to settle for second place.

ITALIAN GRAND PRIX
MONZA

16th

Curva Grande

Variante della Roggia

Curva di Lesmos

Rettifilo Tribune

Curva del Serraglio

Curva del Vialone

Variante Ascari

Curva Parabolica

'00 Pole: M Schumacher
Winner: M Schumacher
Timing sectors

Circuit length. . . . . . . 5.792 km	2000 RESULTS	
Race distance. . . . . . . 53 laps	1 Michael Schumacher	Ferrari
Lap record	2 Mika Hakkinen	McLaren
MIKA HAKKINEN	3 Ralf Schumacher	Williams
(McLaren-Mercedes)	4 Jos Verstappen	Arrows
1m 25.595s, 151.401mph	5 Alexander Wurz	Benetton
2000	6 Ricardo Zonta	BAR

INDIANAPOLIS

ROUND 16: SEPTEMBER 30, 2001

The new-for-Formula One Indianapolis Motor Speedway wowed the sport's insiders with its steeply-banked stretch of track and packed grandstands, but the tight and uninteresting infield section was too twisty to win any prizes.

REVERSE DIRECTION: The Formula One cars tackle the banked section of the regular oval in the opposite direction to that taken by those racing on the oval

America was given its first taste of Formula One for nine years last September when the Indianapolis Motor Speedway was rejigged as never before for the United States Grand Prix. And it was Michael Schumacher who won the hearts of the sell-out crowd that filled the gargantuan grandstands around the world's most famous oval.

Whether the USA has embraced its Grand Prix or not, it has always been a hugely important country for Formula One, especially since sponsorship became the sport's lifeblood. Not surprisingly, the sponsors would clamber over themselves to have access to the world's largest market. Yet their hopes exceeded the impact they made as the US Grand Prix moved to increasingly unimpressive street circuits and interest dwindled. Even races in Detroit, home of the American motor industry, failed to bloom. The race was dropped from the World Championship after a last race at Phoenix in 1991. American fans found Formula One alien. They wanted NASCAR stock cars, something they understood. After all, didn't

NASCAR's good ol' boys hit 230mph on the superspeedways, faster than Formula One cars down the long straights of Hockenheim? For Formula One to hit back, it had to hit back hard, which it did at the Indianapolis Motor Speedway.

A RACE ON THE MOVE

The US Grand Prix didn't join the World Championship until 1959, hosting the title decider at Sebring. Bumpy and potholed, this wasn't popular, so the race reappeared a year later at Riverside in California. This was another one-hit wonder, and the 1961 US Grand Prix was held at Watkins Glen in New York State. More to the liking of the teams and drivers, and better attended too, it was to be the race's home until 1980, by which time the country had been given a second race, the US West Grand Prix held on the streets of Long Beach in California. Other cities opened their streets, with races held at Las Vegas, Detroit, Dallas and finally Phoenix. But, after 1991, Formula One wasn't invited back until 2000.

The race's new home is best known for its 500-mile race, with 400,000 fans packing the grandstands around the 2.5-mile oval. The Indy 500 counted for World Championship points between 1950 and 1960, even though no Formula One cars or drivers took part. Then, just as the Indianapolis 500 was dropped from the World Championship, so Lotus made a push, with their Formula One-derived racers winning in 1965 and 1966 through Jim Clark and Graham Hill respectively, forcing the locals to consign their front-engined roadsters to history.

The Indianapolis 500 slumped in 1996

AN UNUSUAL SENSATION: Mika Hakkinen accelerates his McLaren out of the flat infield section and up onto the banking of what is Turn One for those on the regular oval circuit. For the Formula One racers, this is the last corner of the lap

when the circuit's owner Tony George fell out with the teams and formed the Indy Racing League. The top teams went off and raced in their own championship and George held on to the Indianapolis 500, losing out as the IRL drivers were second rank. George was forced to open the circuit to NASCAR stock cars for the Brickyard 400 to cut his losses. Then he and Formula One's Bernie Ecclestone masterminded this race.

WRONG WAY AROUND

The original Indianapolis Motor Speedway consisted of two straights linked by banked corners. Made of crushed stone when it opened in 1909, its slippery surface led to deaths. This prompted owner Carl Fisher to pave the track with more than three million bricks, thus its nickname "The Brickyard". However, it's now Tarmac-covered with the exception of a strip marking the start/finish line.

A special circuit was built for the arrival of Formula One, with only the start/finish straight and Turn One being used. Running the "wrong" way up the start/finish straight, the track feeds into a tight right/left ess before entering a long, tightening right-hander. A right-hand kink pours the track into an open 180-degree left. This is followed almost immediately by an open right onto a short straight behind the pit garages and paddock. The second twisting section follows, with a left kink into a right-hand hairpin followed by a left-hand hairpin. A longish right turns the track back towards the original circuit, with the drivers bursting back onto the banking just at the entry to Turn Two. Then, alien to Formula One, the track is fast, wide and steeply banked through Turn One back onto the start/finish straight. With that tight first corner addressing them, the drivers were able to go for some great overtaking moves, even if Schumacher found it hard to make his stick on David Coulthard.

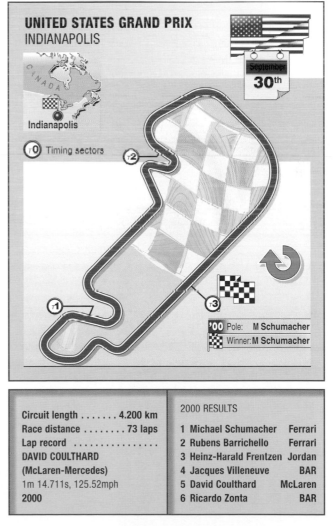

UNITED STATES GRAND PRIX
INDIANAPOLIS

September **30**th

Indianapolis

⓪ Timing sectors

'00 Pole: M Schumacher
Winner: M Schumacher

Circuit length . . . . 4.200 km	2000 RESULTS	
Race distance . . . . 73 laps	1 Michael Schumacher	Ferrari
Lap record	2 Rubens Barrichello	Ferrari
DAVID COULTHARD	3 Heinz-Harald Frentzen	Jordan
(McLaren-Mercedes)	4 Jacques Villeneuve	BAR
1m 14.711s, 125.52mph	5 David Coulthard	McLaren
2000	6 Ricardo Zonta	BAR

SUZUKA

ROUND 17: OCTOBER 14, 2001

Back in its traditional slot as the final Grand Prix of the World Championship this year, Suzuka has the added attraction of being one of the very best circuits visited all year.

EVER TWISTING: The track may twist and turn, but that doesn't stop Michael Schumacher, as shown here as he takes the outside line at the Dunlop Curve

Unsurprisingly for a race that has been traditionally the venue for the last race or penultimate race of the season, the Japanese Grand Prix has been home to some nail-biting shoot-outs, with two between Ayrton Senna and Alain Prost in 1989 and 1990 standing out as races of particular aggression. With its grandstands packed with fanatical supporters, the race at Suzuka is often one of the classic encounters of the year.

Considering Japan's involvement with the world's automotive market from the 1960s and the participation of Honda's Formula One team from 1964, it's amazing that it wasn't until 1976 that Japan hosted a Grand Prix. Even then, its fans enjoyed just two races before Formula One moved on again. It wasn't until 1987 that Japan held its third Grand Prix and became established in the World Championship.

The Japanese Grand Prix's first venue was Fuji Speedway on the slopes of the Mt Fuji volcano. This hosted the title shoot-out between Niki Lauda and James Hunt, but blinding rain encouraged Lauda to withdraw after two laps and Mario Andretti splashed to victory for Lotus, while McLaren's Hunt finished third and this was just enough to give him the title.

A year later, Gilles Villeneuve's Ferrari flew over a fence and killed two people, putting a question-mark over Fuji's suitability. When the Grand Prix re-emerged in 1987, it was held at Suzuka, where it has remained.

DECEPTIVE BENDS

Suzuka is a fast and technical circuit. Experience here counts, as shown by Eddie Irvine, Jacques Villeneuve and Ralf Schumacher who all spent their formative years in Japanese championships, and perform notably well at Suzuka.

The track drops from the grid to the first corner, a double-apex right-hander. Exit speed is crucial as it leads into a tricky series of uphill esses. The Dunlop Curve, a fourth-gear left-hander, is next, then the track continues its gentle climb to Degner Curve, a sixth-gear right-hander that takes the track under a bridge, through a kink into a 40mph left-hand hairpin. A curving, flat-out blast follows to Spoon Curve. This is a long left-hander at the highest point of the circuit and it's crucial to get it right as the corner opens onto the fastest section of the track. Half-way up the straight to the final chicane comes 130R, a sixth-gear corner taken at around 160mph after being approached at 195mph. A shorter straight brings drivers to the final corner, the ultra-tight chicane known as the Casio Triangle at which the majority of overtaking manoeuvres are attempted. Some are even successful... The track then bends right and dips immediately into the start/finish straight.

DRAMA GUARANTEED

Gerhard Berger won on Formula One's first visit to Suzuka in 1987, and a host of top names have won at this tricky and demanding circuit since, with the Austrian being joined as a two-time winner by Ayrton Senna, Damon Hill, Michael Schumacher and

Mika Hakkinen. Last year, of course, Schumacher moved past them all with his third win there.

In 1997, the Japanese Grand Prix was the penultimate race of the World Championship, and it provided drama aplenty even before it started. Villeneuve had arrived with a nine-point advantage over Michael Schumacher, so all he had to do was finish ahead of him to become champion. To do this, first he had to start, and he got himself disqualified from doing so by driving at unabated speed past a waved yellow flag during practice. Only when the Williams team appealed against this decision was he allowed to start, and the race was packed with incident and interesting tactics as Irvine did everything in his power to ensure his Ferrari team-mate took the maximum haul of points.

The Japanese Grand Prix was back to its position as the last one on the calendar in 1998 and Schumacher was again in contention for the title. But he stalled at the start of the parade lap, blowing his chances of starting from his hard-won pole position as that meant he would have to start from the rear of the grid. This handed the title to Mika Hakkinen who was able to relax completely as he raced on to victory and the title. Schumacher's day went from bad to worse as his Ferrari had a blow-out and he retired. Hakkinen did battle again in 1999, but this time with the other Ferrari driver, Irvine. However, he was in control from the start, with Irvine able to finish only a distant third.

Last year's race turned out to be a championship decider, even though it wasn't the last race of the year, as Michael Schumacher and Ferrari worked their tactics perfectly in mixed conditions at the second round of pitstops to overhaul Hakkinen, who had never looked likely to be passed in a straight, on-track manoeuvre. David Coulthard finished a distant third on a day when no-one could live with the pace of the lead duo.

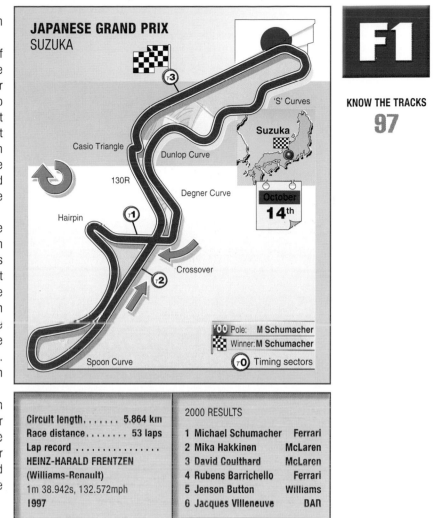

JAPANESE GRAND PRIX
SUZUKA

'S' Curves

Suzuka

October **14**th

Casio Triangle

Dunlop Curve

130R

Degner Curve

Hairpin

Crossover

Spoon Curve

'00 Pole: M Schumacher
Winner: M Schumacher
Timing sectors

Circuit length	5.864 km
Race distance	53 laps
Lap record	
HEINZ-HARALD FRENTZEN	
(Williams-Renault)	
1m 38.942s, 132.572mph	
1997	

2000 RESULTS

1 Michael Schumacher	Ferrari
2 Mika Hakkinen	McLaren
3 David Coulthard	McLaren
4 Rubens Barrichello	Ferrari
5 Jenson Button	Williams
6 Jacques Villeneuve	BAR

HITTING THE APEX: Jacques Villeneuve shows how to take the ultimate line, something that is more critical here than at most tracks. His BAR is shown on the approach to the Crossover

WHEEL-TO-WHEEL: Hakkinen and Michael Schumacher were this close last year

Michael Schumacher fought for four years for Ferrari without achieving his aim of becoming the famous Italian team's first World Champion since Jody Scheckter ended the 1979 campaign on top of the points table. However, that quest was brought to fruition last year when he kept his head in a season that ebbed and flowed between himself and McLaren's Mika Hakkinen and David Coulthard to clinch the title with a round still to run. There were, however, a few other drivers who played a starring role in Schumacher's wake.

Michael Schumacher isn't the best-paid driver in the world for nothing, as he has shown since joining Ferrari in 1996 after claiming two titles for Benetton. The Italian team was struggling, only occasionally improving on midfield positions. Yet, with the German leading the way and the Fiat parent company throwing millions upon millions at it as Jean Todt restructured the team, a corner was there to be turned. Turn it they did, with Schumacher winning 16 times for Ferrari before last season. Then, with Schumacher winning nine races in 2000, they landed their holy grail.

In truth, while people talk of McLaren having had the best car for the past three seasons, many miss the point that the Ferrari was almost its equal in 1999 as Eddie Irvine challenged Hakkinen all the way to the final round. And the cars were certainly on level terms last year when the Ferrari number-two seat was filled by Rubens Barrichello. It was a

AUSTRALIAN GP BRAZILIAN GP SAN MARINO GP BRITISH GP
AUSTRIAN GP GERMAN GP HUNGARIAN GP BELGIAN GP

case of Ferrari and McLaren slugging it out at each of the 17 Grands Prix and the other nine teams fighting over their scraps.

Schumacher had a dream start when he won the first three Grands Prix as McLaren floundered, their unreliability squandering their initial pace advantage. Adding insult to injury, Coulthard was disqualified from second in Brazil. Coulthard won three times by July, in which time his team-mate Hakkinen had won just once, but his challenge faded, while Barrichello read the changeable conditions best at Hockenheim for a hugely popular first win.

Schumacher's season came off the rails at the midway point when his car broke when he was leading at Monaco, his engine failed when he was second at Magny-Cours and he followed this by retiring after first-corner accidents at the A1-Ring and Hockenheim. But a run of two second places and three wins took him to that coveted title with a tactical victory over Hakkinen in the Japanese Grand Prix.

Of the rest, Williams produced the biggest surprise. Jordan was expected to finish third in the Constructors' Cup for a second successive season, even to close the gap to Ferrari and McLaren, but their cars broke too frequently for that. Instead, Williams profited in its first season with BMW as its engine partner, shining when people had expected it to be a development year. Ralf Schumacher gave the folk from Munich a flying start with a surprise third place in the opening round, but it wasn't just Ralf who shone, with rookie Jenson Button impressing enormously after he'd leapt straight from Formula Three. Benetton never matched Giancarlo Fisichella's second place in round two in Brazil, and will be looking forward to having works engines from Renault in 2001. However, BAR clearly made progress in its second season. It even scored points, something that it hadn't managed in 1999. One of the teams over which it climbed on its way to the front was Jaguar (formerly Stewart) which appeared to fall apart

at the seams, although Eddie Irvine and Johnny Herbert both had occasional strong outings.

Sauber continued to be the most anonymous team in Formula One, seldom troubling the scorers and yet not getting as much TV exposure as the cars at the back that appear most frequently when being lapped.

Arrows made strong progress last year and appear to have joined the ranks of midfield teams, leaving Prost to fall to the depths at the back, with Jean Alesi and Nick Heidfeld seldom finishing and usually qualifying ahead of only the Minardis.

Grands Prix that stand out include the British Grand Prix for the Silverstone mud bath; the Italian Grand Prix sadly for the massive first-lap accident that claimed the life of a marshal at the second chicane; the United States Grand Prix for putting Formula One on the banking at Indianapolis; and the Japanese Grand Prix for the release of emotion as Michael Schumacher completed Ferrari's title dream.

ISH GP EUROPEAN GP MONACO GP CANADIAN GP FRENCH GP
IAN GP UNITED STATES GP JAPANESE GP MALAYSIAN GP

F1 THE YEAR IN PICTURES

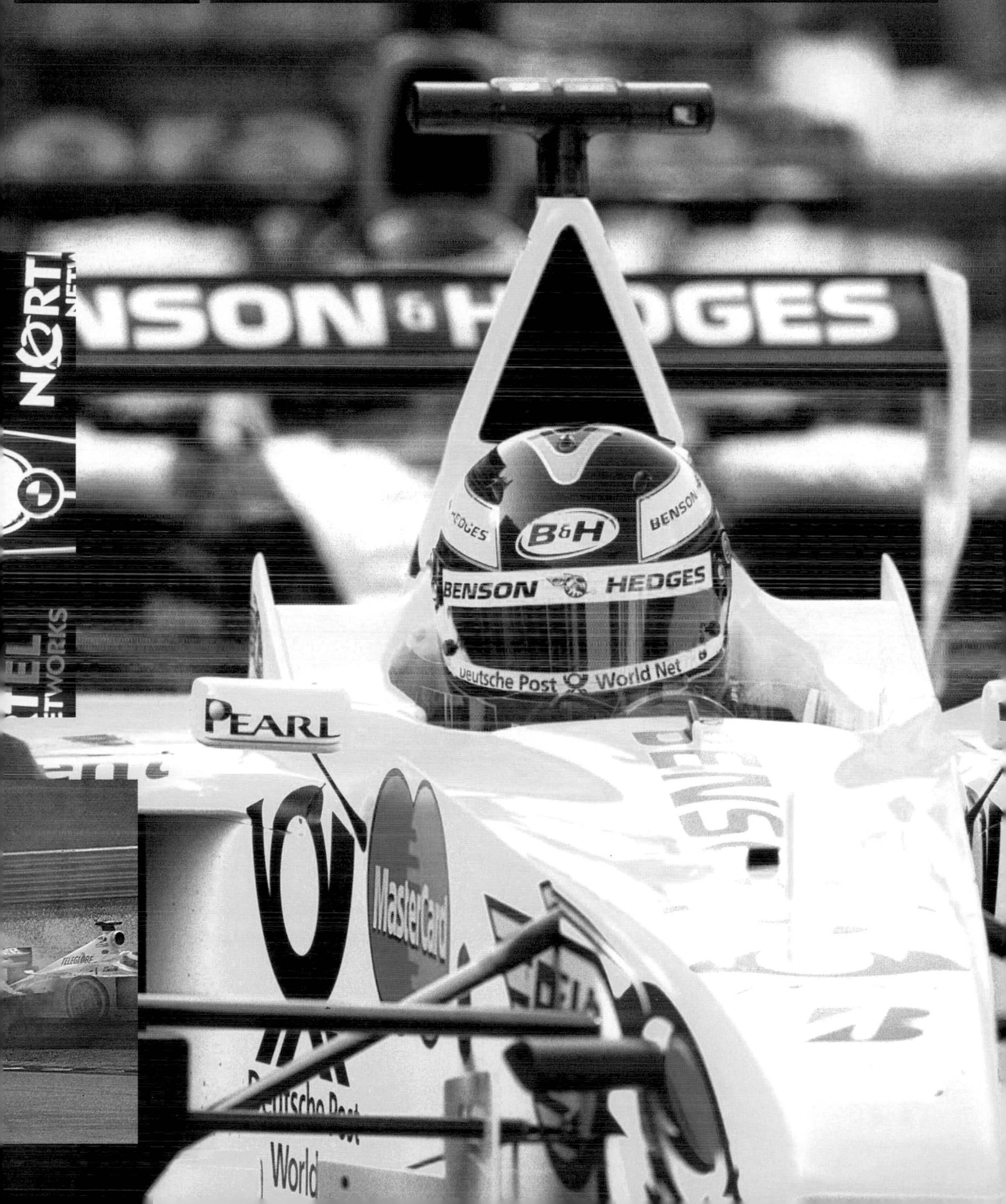

AUSTRALIAN GP

RELIABILITY PAYS

McLaren should have opened their account for 2000 with a one-two result in Melbourne, but both their cars broke down and let Ferrari begin its campaign with maximum points as Michael Schumacher led home Rubens Barrichello.

RACE RESULTS

ROUND 1
AT MELBOURNE, MARCH 12, 2000
58 LAPS – 191.57 MILES

	Driver	Team
1	Michael Schumacher	Ferrari
2	Rubens Barrichello	Ferrari
3	Ralf Schumacher	Williams
4	Jacques Villeneuve	BAR
5	Giancarlo Fisichella	Benetton
6	Ricardo Zonta	BAR

POLE . . . . **Hakkinen**
1m 30.548s (131.32mph/211.33kph)

FASTEST LAP . . . . **Barrichello**
1m 31.481s (129.70mph/208.72kph)

WEATHER . . . . Hot, dry & sunny

AN EMOTIONAL START: Michael Schumacher celebrates his first winning start since 1995 with his team-mate and his brother

'To finish first, first you must finish' is an old adage. But never was it more true than in the season-opening race in Melbourne where McLaren looked to be in control but came away with nothing, just like in 1999. Worse still for McLaren, arch-rivals Ferrari came away with a full complement of points.

Mika Hakkinen qualified his McLaren on pole, with team-mate David Coulthard alongside. The Ferraris of Schumacher and Barrichello were next ahead of the Jordans of Heinz-Harald Frentzen and Jarno Trulli, but none of this quartet could trouble the men in grey at the start. Hakkinen won the run to the first corner and Coulthard tucked in behind, while Frentzen outsprinted Barrichello and slotted into fourth. The Jordans weren't as fast as the Ferraris, so Barrichello fumed as he found himself stuck and had to watch team leader Michael Schumacher chase after the McLarens.

First to crack was Coulthard when his Mercedes engine failed after 11 laps. Just seven laps later, Hakkinen's did the same and the race was Schumacher's, with Frentzen 16 seconds adrift with two-thirds of the race still to run.

And so it was that Schumacher won the season's opening race for the first time since 1995, with Barrichello moving up into second by changing from a one-stop strategy and pitting before Frentzen. Taking on only a little fuel, the Brazilian benefited from a light car and moved into second. He had still to pit again to take on enough fuel to finish the race, but the pressure was relieved when Frentzen's gearbox failed, with Trulli's having expired and led to his retirement a few laps earlier.

The unfancied Williams-BMW combination was given a podium placing on its debut as Ralf Schumacher advanced from eleventh on the grid to third, well clear of a battle between Jacques Villeneuve, Giancarlo Fisichella, Jenson Button, Ricardo Zonta and Mika Salo. However, Button's dream of points on his debut ended when his engine blew, while Salo passed Zonta for sixth only to be disqualified for an illegal front wing. So, after a whole year without a point in 1999, BAR had both of its drivers as scorers in Australia.

BRAZILIAN GP

FAIR AND SQUARE

If his first-round win in Australia was assisted by McLaren's reliability problems, then Michael Schumacher's victory at Interlagos was taken without their assistance, even though rival Hakkinen failed to last the distance.

RACE RESULTS

ROUND 2
AT INTERLAGOS, MARCH 26, 2000

71 LAPS – 190.21 MILES

	Driver	Team
1	Michael Schumacher	Ferrari
2	Giancarlo Fisichella	Benetton
3	Heinz-Harald Frentzen	Jordan
4	Jarno Trulli	Jordan
5	Ralf Schumacher	Williams
6	Jenson Button	Williams

POLE . . . . **Hakkinen**
1m 14.111s (130.13mph/209.42kph)

FASTEST LAP . . . . . **M. Schumacher**
1m 14.755s (128.97mph/207.54kph)

WEATHER . . **Hot & dry but overcast**

Buoyed by his flying start in Australia, Michael Schumacher found himself 0.4 seconds behind pole-sitter Mika Hakkinen in Brazil. However, he made short work of the McLarens, sprinting past David Coulthard before the first corner. Then, a lap later, he was in front, having passed Hakkinen, diving down the inside into the first corner. By now it was clear that the German was running with a lighter fuel load, planning to run a two-stop strategy. The McLarens had opted to run the race with just one stop. Rubens Barrichello also took advantage of the McLarens' load and demoted Coulthard to fourth on lap 2.

Schumacher was 21 seconds ahead of Hakkinen when he made his first pit stop. When he emerged, he was 7 seconds behind the Finn and they both had one stop left to make. So it was race on. However, the fans were deprived of an intriguing battle as Hakkinen spotted his engine's oil pressure was plummeting and pulled off.

Barrichello led for two laps after Schumacher pitted, having passed Hakkinen. However, his stop dropped him back to fourth, and then the grandstands fell quiet five laps later when home-town hero Barrichello slowed and pulled off with hydraulics failure.

And so Schumacher was left to win as he pleased ahead of Coulthard, crossing the line 4 seconds in front. But the Scot was then disqualified as his car's nose wing was found to be 7mm too low, with McLaren blaming bottoming on the circuit's bumps. This was a double blow as he had driven extraordinarily hard to finish so close to the German having lost first, second and third gears early in the race.

Eddie Irvine circulated on his own behind the Ferraris and McLarens, but crashed when he pressed just a little too hard.

Having run with an unusually large amount of ground clearance thus paid off for Benetton's Giancarlo Fisichella who was elevated to second place. He moved ahead of the Jordans by mid-distance, with Heinz-Harald Frentzen completing the podium after overhauling Jarno Trulli when his team-mate pitted for a second stop. Williams grabbed the final points, with Ralf Schumacher fifth and rookie Jenson Button scoring his first points.

OOPS!: Eddie Irvine was set to score Jaguar's first points, but he misread the tactics of others behind him, pressed too hard and crashed out

SAN MARINO GP

SCHUEY MAKES IT THREE

RACE RESULTS

ROUND 3
AT IMOLA, APRIL 9, 2000
62 LAPS – 190.40 MILES

	Driver	Team
1	Michael Schumacher	Ferrari
2	Mika Hakkinen	McLaren
3	David Coulthard	McLaren
4	Rubens Barrichello	Ferrari
5	Jacques Villeneuve	BAR
6	Mika Salo	Sauber

POLE . . . . Hakkinen
1m 24.714s (130.50mph / 210.02kph)

FASTEST LAP . . . . Hakkinen
1m 26.523s (127.56mph / 205.28kph)

WEATHER . . . . . Warm, dry & sunny

Mika Hakkinen scored the first points of his campaign and led for the greatest number of laps but, crucially, he was behind Michael Schumacher's Ferrari when they reached the finish, as the German made it three from three.

Looking back at this race, it's hard to know whether it was more significant for Michael Schumacher and Ferrari overhauling Mika Hakkinen and McLaren in a straight fight, or for Schumacher showing ultra-competitiveness at the start, something that would be seen again later in the year.

As Barrichello delayed Coulthard, the Scot became increasingly frustrated at being trapped behind a slower driver. With everyone planning to stop twice, there was little chance of passing through a superior pit strategy. And it was only when they made their second stops at the same

starts through the season.

HOME WIN: Michael Schumacher makes it three out of three in 2000

On pole for the third race in a row, Hakkinen got away cleanly, but Schumacher was slow off the mark and in order not to lose ground cut across the bows of Coulthard, forcing him to lift – and forcing brother Ralf onto the grass – so that his team-mate Rubens Barrichello could insert himself as a buffer. Schumacher was thus able to remain second, but Coulthard fell to fourth and Ralf Schumacher from fifth to ninth. Coming in the other direction, BAR's Jacques Villeneuve leapt from ninth to fifth in the first of what would be many storming

time that Coulthard nosed ahead, almost wiping the nose off Barrichello's Ferrari as he powered away from his pit slot just in front of it.

Hakkinen eased clear of Schumacher, but he then hit something on the track and damaged his floor, affecting the car's handling. He survived this, but his lead came down from 5 seconds to 2 seconds when first his engine momentarily cut out then Jos Verstappen obstructed him. He then pitted for an early second stop and Schumacher made the most of a clear track

before his own stop. After a quick stop, Schumacher sent the tifosi wild by emerging in front by 3 seconds. Somehow, Schumacher had done it again and collected his third set of maximum points.

The extent to which Barrichello had delayed Coulthard was shown by Coulthard finishing third, fully 50 seconds behind Hakkinen, but almost 40 seconds ahead of the Brazilian. Every other driver had been lapped, with Villeneuve collecting his second points score for BAR with fifth place, chased across the line by Salo.

BRITISH GP

DAVID DOES IT AGAIN

David Coulthard scored his second British GP win in a row, but this time he did so by beating the best, as neither Mika Hakkinen nor Michael Schumacher retired from the race and thus stood below him on the podium.

David Coulthard said before the season started that it was "no more Mr Nice Guy". This year he was going to take the battle to Mika Hakkinen and Michael Schumacher. Many thought that this was little more than hot air, but his showing in the Brazilian GP had indicated that he was serious. That, however, was nothing compared to his drive at Silverstone.

The seemingly relentless rain ceased before qualifying and Rubens Barrichello showed his famed ability on damp surfaces to take pole for Ferrari. He did so in the last minute of a session that saw pole change hands between 11 drivers, pipping Heinz-Harald Frentzen by 0.003 seconds...

Barrichello led away from Frentzen, with Coulthard jumping Hakkinen for third. Michael Schumacher also had a go at Hakkinen but did so with two wheels on the

MY TURN: Coulthard enjoys his victory

wet grass. Slowed by this, he was demoted to eighth by Jenson Button, a fast-starting Jacques Villeneuve and his brother Ralf. Michael had a go back at Ralf into Bridge Corner, but the Williams driver wasn't yielding and held on. A lap later, Ralf put Villeneuve between himself and his brother. Frentzen put the pressure on Barrichello as the first six ran in close order as Villeneuve faded. However, the Canadian was able to keep Ferrari's number one behind him and both were promoted at one-third distance when Frentzen's Jordan and the two Williamses pitted for fuel and tyres.

Right on half distance, Barrichello's Ferrari hiccoughed at Becketts, allowing Coulthard – second after Frentzen's stop – to attack. Using Barrichello's tow down the Hangar Straight, he dived past around the outside into Stowe. Although he lost the lead to Barrichello when he pitted two laps

later, Barrichello spun when a hydraulic problem afflicted his Ferrari.

Making his pit stop later than anyone else, Michael Schumacher took the lead. He then handed over to Frentzen, but the Jordan driver almost immediately came in for his second pit stop, leaving Coulthard with a lead he was never to lose. Likewise, Hakkinen moved into second place when the Williamses pitted for a second time and Michael moved into third. Frentzen's run was ended when his car jammed in sixth gear, but Jordan still managed to score when Villeneuve's transmission failed and Jarno Trulli moved into sixth place behind the two Williams entries.

RACE RESULTS	
ROUND 4	
AT SILVERSTONE, APRIL 23, 2000	
60 LAPS – 191.64 MILES	

	Driver	Team
1	David Coulthard	McLaren
2	Mika Hakkinen	McLaren
3	Michael Schumacher	Ferrari
4	Ralf Schumacher	Williams
5	Jenson Button	Williams
6	Jarno Trulli	Jordan

POLE . . . . Barrichello
1m 25.703s (134.17mph/215.91kph)

FASTEST LAP . . . . Hakkinen
1m 26.217s (133.40mph/214.68kph)

WEATHER . . Cool & cloudy, but dry

SPANISH GP

MCLAREN BACK ON SONG

McLaren's first one-two result of the season gave reigning champion Mika Hakkinen his first reason to smile all year, especially as Michael Schumacher suffered a series of mistakes and failures and collected only two points.

RACE RESULTS

ROUND 5
AT BARCELONA, MAY 7, 2000
65 LAPS – 192.47 MILES

	Driver	Team
1	Mika Hakkinen	McLaren
2	David Coulthard	McLaren
3	Rubens Barrichello	Ferrari
4	Ralf Schumacher	Williams
5	Michael Schumacher	Ferrari
6	Heinz-Harald Frentzen	Jordan

POLE . . . . M. Schumacher
1m 20.974s (131.64mph/211.85kph)

FASTEST LAP . . . . Hakkinen
1m 24.470s (125.99mph/202.75kph)

WEATHER . . . . **Warm, dry & cloudy**

The big news was that David Coulthard had survived a plane crash that killed his pilot and co-pilot. Concealing three cracked ribs, he lapped fastest in Friday and Saturday practice, but his car had a fuel-pressure problem that forced him to qualify with extra fuel on board, ending up fourth as pole position went to Michael Schumacher ahead of Mika Hakkinen and Rubens Barrichello.

The order was jumbled as Barrichello was slow away and Ralf Schumacher sprinted past Coulthard for third. Thus, Coulthard again found himself delayed by a slower car as Michael Schumacher and Hakkinen escaped. Pedro Diniz spun off on the opening lap, followed by Pedro de la Rosa cannoning into Jean Alesi.

Just as the first round of pit stops commenced, Jacques Villeneuve retired from sixth place. But this was nothing compared to what happened at Michael Schumacher's first pit stop, when he was signalled away before his chief mechanic Nigel Stepney had disconnected the refuelling hose. As a result Michael ran over him. So, although Michael was able to rejoin in a position to be in the lead after Hakkinen had made his stop, Ferrari would have to find a refueller for Barrichello's visit in a lap's time. This went alright, but Schumacher's second stop wasn't so smooth and Hakkinen, who made his second stop on the same lap, came out ahead as the new refueller made a mess of engaging the hose and cost him 10 seconds.

Coulthard failed to engage first gear at his stop and fell to fifth. However, he pitted a lap before Ralf Schumacher and Barrichello for his second stop, and was able to nip past Ralf as the Williams driver rejoined from his second stop, going around the outside... With a clear track, he set off after Michael's Ferrari. It looked to be futile, but Michael had a puncture. Coulthard caught him and was chopped as he went down the inside into the first corner. A lap later, he passed on the outside. Michael was then caught by Ralf and Barrichello. Displaying no brotherly love, he pushed Ralf wide into Banc Sabadell, allowing Barrichello to dive past both. Michael then pitted and fell to fifth. Heinz-Harald Frentzen was the only other unlapped runner, bringing his Jordan home sixth, elevated with four laps to go as Jenson Button's engine blew.

ACTION TIME: Michael Schumacher leads from Hakkinen and his brother

EUROPEAN GP

SCHUEY WINS AT HOME

If it rains, look to Michael Schumacher and you won't go far wrong if you're picking a likely winner. And this is what happened early in this race at his home circuit as he caught and passed Mika Hakkinen to score his fourth win.

RACE RESULTS

ROUND 6
AT NURBURGRING, MAY 21, 2000
67 LAPS – 189.68 MILES

	Driver	Team
1	Michael Schumacher	Ferrari
2	Mika Hakkinen	McLaren
3	David Coulthard	McLaren
4	Rubens Barrichello	Ferrari
5	Giancarlo Fisichella	Benetton
6	Pedro de la Rosa	Arrows

POLE . . . . Coulthard
1m 17.529s (131.46mph/211.55kph)

FASTEST LAP . . . . . M. Schumacher
1m 22.269s (124.60mph/200.52kph)

WEATHER . . . . Cool & dry then wet

David Coulthard won plaudits the length of the pitlane when he claimed pole position. Not only did it mark his first pole in two years, but it showed that he had put his injuries from his plane crash before demoted by guess who? Yes, Jacques Villeneuve who made yet another blinding start, going from ninth to fifth place before the pack had reached the first corner.

Hakkinen and Michael Schumacher eased

the previous Grand Prix behind him and came as a perfect response to comments from team-mate Hakkinen that he would never be as fast as the Finn. Hakkinen, as it happens, was only third fastest behind Michael Schumacher.

However, Hakkinen had the last laugh as he made a scorcher of a start and shot between the front-row men at the start. Coulthard dropped to third, just resisting a challenge from Rubens Barrichello.

As always at the Nurburgring, there was trouble at the first corner as Benetton's Giancarlo Fisichella clashed with Jarno Trulli, leaving the Jordan driver as the race's first retirement. They had already been

clear from Coulthard and Barrichello when rain started to fall after five laps. Then Michael Schumacher dived past the Finnish driver into the Veedol-S on lap 11. He then put the hammer down and pulled clear as Hakkinen teetered on the increasingly wet track. Then it was time for rain tyres. And those who stayed out even for a single extra lap lost a lot of time. Coulthard had pitted a lap before Hakkinen and emerged second, with the Finn third. But Hakkinen soon corrected that.

Michael Schumacher came in for his second stop on lap 35. Hakkinen waited another ten laps, but the lap before he came in he was blocked and lost 3 seconds. This

SHOOTING ARROWS: De la Rosa shone in wet conditions, climbing from 12th place to third before finishing sixth

meant that Schumacher had passed the pit exit and entered the first corner before Hakkinen re-emerged. So, it was race over as Michael made it four wins from six starts.

Coulthard was the best of the rest, but was lapped in the process, winning his battle with Barrichello who was forced by Ferrari to run a three-stop race, something with which the Brazilian was less than happy. Fifth place went to Giancarlo Fisichella 12 seconds further back with Pedro de la Rosa showing strong form to take sixth.

MONACO GP

PATIENCE PAYS OFF

Michael Schumacher was away and clear for Ferrari, but then his rear suspension collapsed and David Coulthard was there to steal the spoils for his first win around the streets of Monaco.

RACE RESULTS

ROUND 7
AT MONACO, JUNE 4, 2000
78 LAPS – 163.72 MILES

	Driver	Team
1	David Coulthard	McLaren
2	Rubens Barrichello	Ferrari
3	Giancarlo Fisichella	Benetton
4	Eddie Irvine	Jaguar
5	Mika Salo	Sauber
6	Mika Hakkinen	McLaren

POLE . . . . M. Schumacher
1m 19.475s (95.08mph/153.01kph)

FASTEST LAP . . . . Hakkinen
1m 21.571s (92.44mph/148.75kph)

WEATHER . . . . . Warm, dry & sunny

NO SPACE TO MOVE: The most anachronistic part of this circuit is the curving and crowded pitlane. Here Frentzen has little space to move as he leaves

The great drivers tend to win at Monaco, and Michael Schumacher looked to be heading for his fifth win in the principality. But it was not to be. He appeared to have matters totally under control, as he had claimed the pole position that is so critical at Monaco. Better still, arch-rival Mika Hakkinen was starting down in fifth – having been 17th until his final run thanks to crashed cars blocking his previous flying laps – with Jarno Trulli lining up second for Jordan. And the race ran according to the Ferrari ace's plans as Trulli held on to second place and then bottled up the field behind him. Coulthard could do nothing about it as Schumacher loped clear. Coulthard was trailed by Heinz-Harald Frentzen and Hakkinen.

With one-stop strategies the plan for most teams, little was expected to happen until mid-distance. Hakkinen was the first to pit, but it was a lengthy stop to retrieve something that had fallen behind his brake pedal. He rejoined in 13th place. On that very same lap, Trulli's gearbox failed and Coulthard charged after Schumacher like a man possessed. It wasn't likely to yield anything, but no-one appeared to have told him otherwise as he set a string of fastest laps.

Then, 13 laps later, Schumacher made his planned stop without trouble and came out 7 seconds ahead of Coulthard who still had to pit. But the Scot lopped 3 seconds off that and was just set to pit when Schumacher's suspension collapsed. Some said this was due to contact with the barriers, Ferrari claiming that a leaking exhaust had weakened it. Either way, Coulthard was now way out front and duly raced to 10 championship points.

Frentzen's hopes of finishing in second place came to nought when he joined the list of those who ended their race against the Ste Devote barriers with just eight laps to go. So, a grateful Barrichello finished as runner-up, with Giancarlo Fisichella crossing the line third. The Jaguar Racing team finally had something to crow about as Eddie Irvine finished fourth to score the new team's first Championship points, with Mika Salo yet again scoring points at Monaco in fifth. Despite gearbox problems that led to him being lapped, Hakkinen made it back up the order to claim the final point.

CANADIAN GP

FERRARI ALL THE WAY

Michael Schumacher left Canada with his fifth win of the year and a welcome 22-point lead. It shouldn't have been that easy, but he was given an almost clear run when David Coulthard was given a stop-go penalty for an infringement.

RACE RESULTS

F1

ROUND 8

AT MONTREAL, JUNE 18, 2000

69 LAPS – 189.54 MILES

REVIEW OF THE 2000 SEASON

109

	Driver	Team
1	Michael Schumacher	Ferrari
2	Rubens Barrichello	Ferrari
3	Giancarlo Fisichella	Benetton
4	Mika Hakkinen	McLaren
5	Jos Verstappen	Arrows
6	Jarno Trulli	Jordan

POLE . . . . M. Schumacher
1m 18.439s (126.08mph/202.89kph)

FASTEST LAP . . . . Hakkinen
1m 19.049s (125.13mph/201.37kph)

WEATHER . . . . Cool, overcast & dry, wet later

The pattern was becoming set by the time the teams arrived in Montreal: the battle for outright honours was no longer between Michael Schumacher and Mika Hakkinen, but between Schumacher and David Coulthard, with the German 12 points ahead. True to form, Schumacher put his Ferrari on pole, with Coulthard alongside, Rubens Barrichello third and Hakkinen fourth.

As the cars set off on their formation lap, Coulthard stalled. Thus his mechanics had to fire up his engine. But they did this after a 15-second board had been shown, earning him a stop-go penalty.

At the start, Schumacher led away from Coulthard, with Jacques Villeneuve demoting Barrichello, Hakkinen and Heinz-Harald Frentzen to fill third place. This helped those in front, as Schumacher and Coulthard had a 3-second advantage at the end of the first lap.

Coulthard felt confident that he was faster than Schumacher, but he knew that he had to pit for his stop-and-go. He came in on lap 14, re-emerging in tenth place. Pedro de la Rosa demoted Frentzen from sixth place on lap 2 to move onto Hakkinen's tail. However, he pitted early and lost position. Then Barrichello passed Villeneuve on lap 25 and raced after Schumacher who was 30 seconds clear. However, when Schumacher pitted at half-distance, Ferrari noticed that he had a rear brake problem and advised him to back off. Barrichello then opened out a 10-second lead before he pitted again on lap 43.

It started to rain two laps later and he had to pit again, for wet tyres. Had he been able to fit wets straight away, the race would have been his. As it was, Schumacher was able to hold onto the lead, albeit backing off so much that he won by only 0.174 seconds. Coulthard was similarly grieved that he hadn't had wets fitted. Showing them how it should have been done, Benetton put Giancarlo Fisichella straight onto wets on lap 44, helping him from seventh to third ahead of Hakkinen. Fifth went to Jos Verstappen who pushed his Arrows ahead of Alexander Wurz and Trulli, with Coulthard moving onto Trulli's tail by the finish, being helped past Ralf Schumacher when Villeneuve dived past the

Scot into the hairpin and took out the Williams driver with four laps to go.

FAST STARTER, SLOW RACER: Jacques Villeneuve gained three places at the start, but then delayed Barrichello and Hakkinen for the first half of the race

FRENCH GP

COULTHARD THE HARD MAN

Michael Schumacher is seen by many as the hard man of Formula One. But at Magny-Cours it was the turn of David Coulthard to outmuscle the German to claim his third win and close the points gap.

RACE RESULTS

ROUND 9
AT MAGNY-COURS, JULY 2, 2000
72 LAPS – 190.08 MILES

	Driver	Team
1	David Coulthard	McLaren
2	Mika Hakkinen	McLaren
3	Rubens Barrichello	Ferrari
4	Jacques Villeneuve	BAR
5	Ralf Schumacher	Williams
6	Jarno Trulli	Jordan

POLE . . . . M. Schumacher
1m 15.632s (125.74mph/202.34kph)

FASTEST LAP . . . . Coulthard
1m 19.479s (119.65mph/192.55kph)

WEATHER . . . . . Warm, dry & sunny

The difference between David Coulthard and Michael Schumacher had been 12 points before the Canadian GP. Arriving at Magny-Cours, the Scot was 22 points adrift and only victory would really suffice – preferably victory with Schumacher not scoring.

Fastest in the untimed practice sessions, Coulthard looked good for pole. However, his car was sidelined with fuel-pump problems, and it was only when his own was repaired for the final minutes that he was able to go for it. By then, the track had heated up and no-one was able to improve, but he grabbed second behind Schumacher, with Rubens Barrichello third and Hakkinen again fourth.

Schumacher made a weakish start and, as at Imola, pulled across on Coulthard. Not only did this force the McLaren driver to lift, but it allowed Barrichello to get a run on him around the outside, so Ferrari were one-two.

Barrichello wasn't able to keep up with his team leader, but he was able to keep Coulthard at bay. And so Schumacher opened out a 5-second advantage after ten laps. The order behind was static once Jacques Villeneuve had made his customary good start, climbing past Ralf Schumacher and Eddie Irvine to be fifth.

On lap 22, Coulthard dived inside Barrichello at the Adelaide Hairpin. The first round of pit stops followed and Coulthard emerged 5 seconds down on Schumacher and closing. By lap 34, he was close enough to have a go at Schumacher, trying around the outside at Adelaide. Schumacher pulled across on the exit and Coulthard signalled his displeasure with a gesture. Six laps later, with Hakkinen on his tail, Coulthard went up the inside at the same point and this time it worked.

Hakkinen, however, was unable to find a way by Schumacher. But he was gifted second place after the second round of pit stops when Schumacher arrived at the Adelaide hairpin crossed up and Hakkinen dived through. Schumacher then slowed with a blown engine. And so Coulthard gave McLaren its first win here since the French GP moved to Magny-Cours in 1991.

Barrichello endured a slow second pit stop but still claimed third place, while Villeneuve warded off a fast-closing Ralf Schumacher to take fourth place for BAR, with Trulli taking the final point.

CLOSE ACTION: David Coulthard and Michael Schumacher had a few wheel-to-wheel moments at the hairpin

AUSTRIAN GP

WINNING AND LOSING

McLaren came away from Austria with first and second, but the FIA later confiscated winner Hakkinen's 10 points from McLaren's haul, while Michael Schumacher was out at the first corner.

RACE RESULTS

F1

ROUND 10
AT A1-RING, JULY 16, 2000
71 LAPS – 191.42 MILES

REVIEW OF THE 2000 SEASON
111

	Driver	Team
1	Mika Hakkinen	McLaren
2	David Coulthard	McLaren
3	Rubens Barrichello	Ferrari
4	Jacques Villeneuve	BAR
5	Jenson Button	Williams
6	Mika Salo	Sauber

POLE . . . . Hakkinen
1m 10.410s (137.44mph)

FASTEST LAP . . . . Coulthard
1m 11.783s (134.81mph)

WEATHER . . . . . Warm, dry & bright

Mika Hakkinen had departed the previous round at Magny-Cours with those close to him saying that he had seemed jaded all weekend as team-mate David Coulthard showed him the way home, and needed a break. So, he was excused testing and promotional duties and arrived at the A1-Ring refreshed. Whether his loss of form had been due to tiredness or to chasing a non-productive chassis set-up will remain a mystery, but he duly claimed his first pole position since the third round, with Coulthard making it an all silver-grey front row.

The second row was all red, but as the McLarens powered away from the tight first corner, there was trouble in their wake. Michael Schumacher went for the slippery inside line to pull alongside team-mate Rubens Barrichello, who had to adjust his line to avoid contact, and their joint slowing-down caught out Ricardo Zonta and Jarno Trulli, with the BAR driver tipping Schumacher into a spin. Trulli clipped Barrichello and then Schumacher, while Giancarlo Fisichella was hit hard by Pedro Diniz, leaving Schumacher, Trulli and Fisichella out on the spot and the order scrambled.

Much to Schumacher's disappointment, his Ferrari was cleared from the track before the field came around again, so there would be no re-start. Hakkinen and Coulthard then eased away at the front as Mika Salo briefly held third ahead of Pedro de la Rosa and Johnny Herbert. The man on the move was Barrichello, despite a damaged floor, climbing from eighth to fourth. But he could do nothing about de la Rosa's Arrows, which stayed ahead until lap 32 when its gearbox failed.

Hakkinen pulled away from Coulthard, who admitted that he eased off when he realized that there was nothing he could do about the Finn, the six points for second worth all the more with championship leader Michael Schumacher not scoring.

By the time Hakkinen pitted, he had lapped all but Coulthard and Barrichello. Pitting latest of all was Jacques Villeneuve,

GOING NOWHERE FAST: Michael Schumacher's race lasted only as far as the first corner on the first lap when he went off into the gravel after a tap from Zonta

who brought his BAR in on lap 49 in fourth place and emerged in the same position thanks to a couple of fast laps that ensured that Jenson Button didn't get back ahead. The young Williams driver had his mirrors full of Salo and Herbert, but hung on until the chequered flag.

An official seal from Hakkinen's ECU was found to be missing after the race, and the FIA decided the following week that all was correct and that he would keep his points, but that McLaren would lose his 10 points from their Constructors' Cup tally and have to part with $50,000.

GERMAN GP

FROM BACK TO FRONT

RACE RESULTS

ROUND 11
AT HOCKENHEIM, JULY 30, 2000

45 LAPS – 190.85 MILES

	Driver	Team
1	Rubens Barrichello	Ferrari
2	Mika Hakkinen	McLaren
3	David Coulthard	McLaren
4	Jenson Button	Williams
5	Mika Salo	Sauber
6	Pedro de la Rosa	Arrows

POLE . . . . Coulthard
1m 45.697s (144.45mph)

FASTEST LAP . . . . Barrichello
1m 44.300s (146.38mph)

WEATHER . . . Cool & dry, rain later

Rubens Barrichello's German GP weekend was one of extremes. But if the Saturday was its nadir, then the Sunday was definitely its zenith as the Brazilian raced from 18th on the grid to his first Grand Prix win.

Heavy rain was the principal feature of the German Grand Prix from the Friday to the Sunday, with rain falling just before the start of qualifying, and each of the 22 cars raced out to set a time.

corner. This didn't leave Coulthard in the lead, though. Rather Mika Hakkinen had made a blinding start from fourth. Jarno Trulli was third and Pedro de la Rosa fourth. Barrichello was on a charge, though, climbing

SPLASHING TO VICTORY: Barrichello mastered the dry-wet-dry conditions to race to an emotional first Grand Prix win

They struggled on their "dry" tyres and were amazed that David Coulthard had beaten the next best driver by 1.4 seconds in that one flier. It was only right at the end that Schumacher pushed Giancarlo Fisichella back to the second row, ending up 1.366 seconds slower than Coulthard. Barrichello wound up 18th after his car had broken, and the spare chassis wasn't ready until late in the hour.

Coulthard emulated some of Schumacher's tactics at the start and pulled across to the inside line. So Schumacher went to the outside. Unfortunately, this left Fisichella with nowhere to go and they collided. For the second race in a row, neither of these drivers had managed to make it around the first

to third before he confirmed that he was on a two-stop strategy by pitting. The McLarens were planning to stop only once.

Just after mid-distance, a spectator broke onto the track before the Clark Kurve. He ran across the track and proceeded to walk along the grass verge, forcing the safety car to be deployed. And this, in an instant, changed the outcome of the race. Unaware of the problem, Coulthard saw Hakkinen jink into the pit. This was the lap on which the Scot had been due to make his pit stop, but with Hakkinen pitting, he stayed out and came upon the safety car. All those behind had pitted and he had to endure a slow lap before he could pit. The team did

well to get him back out in sixth, but his race was run.

Hakkinen remained in front, ahead of Barrichello, but it poured with rain with just 12 laps to go. Trouble was, this was only in the stadium section and not at the far end of the track. Some found their cars a nightmare on dry tyres on the wet sections, such as Ricardo Zonta who slid out of fourth, while others found them tolerable and stayed out. Hakkinen pitted from the lead and although he was gaining ground when he rejoined on wets and climbed to second, it wasn't enough. Likewise Coulthard, who made it back to third. But the man of the day was Barrichello, who stayed out and recorded his first Grand Prix win at his 124th start.

HUNGARIAN GP

MIKA'S MASTERCLASS

This was a race that looked set to be contested between Michael Schumacher and David Coulthard. However, Mika Hakkinen had other ideas, and blasted past both of them at the start of the race before going on to dominate.

Out of sorts through practice and then through qualifying, Mika Hakkinen just couldn't find a balance for his McLaren around the twists and turns of the Hungaroring. But he scrabbled his way to third on the grid with his last flying lap. Schumacher and Coulthard looked far more in control as they filled the front row. Race-morning warm-up saw Hakkinen only fifth, with Coulthard fastest. So people looked to the Scot as a possible winner, especially as the McLarens were expected to be less tyre-hungry than the Ferrari. However, Coulthard was starting from the dusty side of the track closer to the pit wall – the side off the racing line – so he would be at a disadvantage when trying to put the power down at the start. Hakkinen was starting on the cleaner racing line, and made a start as blinding as the one a fortnight before at Hockenheim, blasting between pole-sitter Schumacher and a slow-starting Coulthard. Down to the first corner, he pulled level with Schumacher, but was on the inside line and so was able to take the lead. Schumacher tucked in behind, while Coulthard was forced to ride it out around the first corner wheel-to-wheel with Ralf Schumacher's Williams. He emerged ahead by the time they entered turn 2. And so the pattern was set for the afternoon.

With the Williams driver delaying Barrichello, the first three escaped, with Hakkinen driving every lap as though it were a qualifying lap. He had changed his car's set-up and it had been transformed.

The first stops came and went without a change of order between the front three, while Ferrari worked it so that Barrichello took on very little fuel and the time saved helped him to emerge ahead of Ralf

Schumacher for fourth. Ralf's brother Michael struggled on his middle stint and Coulthard caught right up with him. However, hopes of passing the Ferrari driver for a McLaren one-two were thwarted by both Minardi drivers failing to pull over to let him lap them, costing time just when he needed it most as he tried to make up ground during the second pit-stop sequence, emerging right on the tail of the German's Ferrari after his own second stop. He would end the race just half a second behind and very frustrated.

With temperatures soaring as it always does in Hungary, it was extremely hot work for the drivers, with Barrichello in particular trouble as his water bottle stopped working

at half-distance and he had to be treated for heat exhaustion after finishing fourth, half a dozen seconds ahead of Ralf Schumacher. The final point went to Heinz-Harald Frentzen, with his Jordan team-mate Jarno Trulli climbing from 12th to seventh by stopping only once.

MAN ON A MISSION: Hakkinen leads the way into the second corner on lap one, leaving Michael Schumacher, David Coulthard and Ralf Schumacher in his wake

RACE RESULTS

ROUND 12
AT HUNGARORING, AUGUST 13, 2000
77 LAPS – 190.195 MILES

	Driver	Team
1	Mika Hakkinen	McLaren
2	Michael Schumacher	Ferrari
3	David Coulthard	McLaren
4	Rubens Barrichello	Ferrari
5	Ralf Schumacher	Williams
6	Heinz-Harald Frentzen	Jordan

POLE . . . . M. Schumacher
1m 17.514s (114.72mph/184.61kph)

FASTEST LAP . . . . Hakkinen
1m 20.028s (111.11mph/178.81kph)

WEATHER . . . Very hot, dry & bright

BELGIAN GP

HAKKINEN'S BLINDING MOVE

RACE RESULTS

ROUND 13
AT SPA-FRANCORCHAMPS, AUGUST 27, 2000
44 LAPS – 190.52 MILES

Driver	Team
1 Mika Hakkinen	McLaren
2 Michael Schumacher	Ferrari
3 Ralf Schumacher	Williams
4 David Coulthard	McLaren
5 Jenson Button	Williams
6 Heinz-Harald Frentzen	Jordan

POLE . . . . **Hakkinen**
1m 50.646s (140.88mph / 226.71kph)

FASTEST LAP . . . . **Barrichello**
1m 53.803s (136.97mph / 220.42kph)

WEATHER . . . . **Overcast & wet, drying later**

It's not often that a driver spins and yet wins. But Hakkinen did, throwing in an overtaking move of blinding brilliance to demote a stunned Michael Schumacher to the runner-up slot.

Few who saw Hakkinen's pass on Michael Schumacher with four laps to go will forget it. Not only did he dive up the inside of the Ferrari into Les Combes, but he did so after squeezing his McLaren up the narrow side of Zonta's BAR as they lapped him. Zonta, unaware of Hakkinen – having seen only Schumacher approaching in his mirrors – could easily have given the German an extra foot of space and tipped the Finn onto the grass and oblivion. It was the defining moment of the 2000 season.

ALL IN A SPIN: Jarno Trulli points the wrong way at the La Source hairpin after being tapped by Jenson Button

The clerk of the course decided that the track surface was wet enough – even though it had stopped raining two hours before – to start the race behind the safety car. In a stroke, the best chance of overtaking was removed, with poleman Hakkinen streaking into a clear lead when the safety car withdrew after one lap.

Trulli held on to an excellent second. But it wasn't to last, with Button making a mistake behind him that let Michael Schumacher through at the Bus Stop on lap 3. By the time this trio reached La Source, Schumacher dived past the Italian and Button decided to go for a gap on

the inside. It wasn't large enough and he hit Trulli, putting the Jordan out of the race and losing enough momentum to allow Coulthard and team-mate Ralf Schumacher past too.

Tyres then became a matter for concern. Pedro Diniz alone had started on dry-weather tyres, soon falling back from 15th to last, but he started to gather speed and on lap 4 Alesi came in for some of the same. He was then clearly faster than anyone else, so everyone came in on lap 6 – everyone except the McLarens, that is, as Hakkinen pitted on lap 7, but Coulthard was left out until lap 8, a decision that would drop him to ninth.

When the order settled, Hakkinen was still in front, from Schumachers Michael and Ralf, Alesi (proving the value of his early change), Button and Villeneuve. Lap 13 proved unlucky for Hakkinen, as he spun at Stavelot and Schumacher's Ferrari went past before he rejoined from the grass.

McLaren made a change to Hakkinen's car at his second stop, and he then hauled in Schumacher so much that he was able to attack into Les Combes on lap 40, where he was chopped by Schumacher, something about which he was less than happy. This mattered for little, as on lap 41 he made that astonishing move and raced off to victory.

Of the rest, poor Alesi's Prost failed and so did Barrichello's Ferrari, helping Frentzen claim the final point for Jordan.

ITALIAN GP

GLORY FOR THE TIFOSI

Last year's Italian Grand Prix won't be remembered for Schumacher's win that moved him level with Ayrton Senna's career total of 41 Grand Prix wins, but for the six-car pile-up on the first lap that led to the death of a marshal.

ROUND 14
AT MONZA, SEPTEMBER 10, 2000
53 LAPS – 190.623 MILES

	Driver	Team
1	Michael Schumacher	Ferrari
2	Mika Hakkinen	McLaren
3	Ralf Schumacher	Williams
4	Jos Verstappen	Arrows
5	Alexander Wurz	Benetton
6	Ricardo Zonta	BAR

POLE . . . . M. Schumacher, 1m 23.770s (154.70mph/248.95kph)

FASTEST LAP . . . . Hakkinen 1m 25.595s (151.40mph/243.65kph)

WEATHER . . . . . . Hot, dry & bright

FOLLOW THE LEADER: The Safety Car ran for 10 laps as the debris from the massive first lap accident at the second chicane was cleared up

If Schumacher had believed the newspapers, he wouldn't have turned up to the race at all, as the accepted script was that he would trail the McLarens. But turn up he did, and he left at the end with 10 points to put him just two points behind Hakkinen. No wonder he broke down with the emotion of it all.

The pre-event talk was also of revisions to the chicanes. With the first one changed to a much tighter single chicane, rather than a shallow pair, an accident was predicted for lap one. Miraculously, all the front runners got through without trouble, with Schumacher leading from Hakkinen and a fast-starting Coulthard, as team-mate Rubens Barrichello lost ground. There was trouble further back, but it eliminated only Eddie Irvine's Jaguar.

This was nothing to what happened at the second chicane as Heinz-Harald Frentzen clipped Barrichello, then his own team-mate Jarno Trulli. All three collected Coulthard. With debris flying everywhere, Pedro de la Rosa clipped Johnny Herbert's Jaguar and his car shot skywards, bouncing over Coulthard's car in the gravel trap before coming to rest inverted practically on top of Barrichello's Ferrari. Amazingly, all emerged uninjured, but an errant wheel had struck and tragically killed a marshal.

The race went on behind the safety car until lap 10, when it indicated that it was pulling off. The field accelerated down the back straight, then Schumacher slowed it down – catching out sixth-placed Jenson Button, who swerved onto the grass to avoid hitting those ahead and crashed out of the race.

With fuel saved, everyone would need to stop just once for fuel, save for Ricardo Zonta who was carrying a light load and would need two visits. His progress was stunning as he climbed from 17th into the points. But then he had to do it all again, twice...

Schumacher eased away from Hakkinen. The Finn flew after his pit stop, but it wasn't enough and Schumacher's win sent the 130,000-strong crowd into paroxysms of delight as they invaded the track.

Jacques Villeneuve ran in third place, lucky that a poor start had put him behind that second chicane accident. But his luck ran out when his BAR's electrics failed. This left Ralf Schumacher to occupy the position for his third Monza podium visit in three years.

A clutch problem during his pit stop cost Giancarlo Fisichella a minute and handed fourth place to Jos Verstappen, whose Arrows showed exceptional straight-line speed. Alexander Wurz scored the first points of his campaign for fifth, with Zonta right on his tail at the chequered flag, wishing that he'd been able to pit just once.

UNITED STATES GP

ADVANTAGE SCHUMACHER

Michael Schumacher always enjoys a win, but with Mika Hakkinen faltering, this one was worth double as he closed in on his third title.

HEADING FOR VICTORY: Michael Schumacher laid down the first marker with the enthusiastic American fans by winning on Formula One's long-awaited return to the United States of America

RACE RESULTS

ROUND 15
AT INDIANAPOLIS,
SEPTEMBER 24, 2000
73 LAPS – 190.15 MILES

	Driver	Team
1	Michael Schumacher	Ferrari
2	Rubens Barrichello	Ferrari
3	Heinz-Harald Frentzen	Jordan
4	Jacques Villeneuve	BAR
5	David Coulthard	McLaren
6	Ricardo Zonta	BAR

POLE . . . . M. Schumacher
1m 14.266s (126.27mph / 203.20kph)

FASTEST LAP . . . . Coulthard
1m 14.711s (125.52mph / 201.99kph)

WEATHER . Cool & damp, but drying

This was the race in which Michael Schumacher and Ferrari pushed their noses in front in the race for the World Championship. It was also the race in which Formula One re-introduced itself to America. Whether it passed muster with the hard-to-please American fans will only be shown by ticket sales when the race returns this September, but they were certainly deprived of a great race by two events involving McLaren's drivers.

Schumacher stuck his Ferrari on pole. However, he was joined on the front row not by title rival Hakkinen but by David Coulthard, who was given a tow to get him there by the driver he usurped: teammate Hakkinen. Insiders reckoned that Coulthard was to be used as a "hare".

Coulthard gave McLaren its first upset when he moved before the red starting lights were extinguished. It helped him pass Schumacher for the lead, but it also earned him a 10-second stop-go penalty. So, once in front, Coulthard slowed the pace to allow Hakkinen to move onto Schumacher's tail. But just as he achieved this, the German fought his way into the lead after some robust jousting from both drivers. Coulthard then dutifully pulled over to let Hakkinen mount his attack.

With the weather having been mixed, it was no surprise that it would play a role. The rain had stopped before the race, but the track was still sufficiently wet for the drivers to start on wet tyres. However, it dried quickly and most drivers pitted for regular tyres after seven or eight laps. Minardi elected to keep Gaston Mazzacane out for longer though, and he rose to fourth. While this was great exposure for the Argentinian, it became clear that perhaps wet tyres were still the ones to have as he kept Hakkinen's dry-shod McLaren at bay for several laps...

At the front of the field, Hakkinen was on a charge and hauling Schumacher in by a second per lap. It wasn't to be though as his engine blew just past one-third distance, and Schumacher was left free to win as he pleased, and to open out an eight-point championship lead.

Behind him, his brother Ralf inherited second, but it was not to be Williams' day as his engine failed – as did that of Jenson Button, who had already clashed again with Jarno Trulli. Heinz-Harald Frentzen then gave Jordan reason to smile as he moved into second, but it wasn't to last as Rubens Barrichello usurped him, leaving Frentzen to fight all the way to the finish to remain in third place ahead of BAR's Jacques Villeneuve. Coulthard's stop-go penalty dropped him to 16th, but he made it back to fifth, kicking himself for his early getaway.

JAPANESE GP

FERRARI COMPLETES ITS DREAM

Jody Scheckter's 21-year reign as Ferrari's most recent World Champion came to an end when Michael Schumacher wrapped up the Championship title with victory at Suzuka.

RACE RESULTS

F1

ROUND 16
AT SUZUKA, OCTOBER 8, 2000
53 LAPS – 193.00 MILES

REVIEW OF THE 2000 SEASON

117

	Driver	Team
1	Michael Schumacher	Ferrari
2	Mika Hakkinen	McLaren
3	David Coulthard	McLaren
4	Rubens Barrichello	Ferrari
5	Jenson Button	Williams
6	Jacques Villeneuve	BAR

POLE . . . . M. Schumacher
1m 35.825s (136.90mph/220.30kph)

FASTEST LAP . . . . Hakkinen
1m 39.189s (132.25mph/212.83kph)

WEATHER . . . . Cool & overcast,
light rain mid-race

This was the race that gave Ferrari fans the world over the result it had been waiting for since 1979: a Ferrari driver as World Champion for the first time since Jody Scheckter's reign.

Michael Schumacher came to the Japanese GP with an eight-point advantage over Mika Hakkinen, anxious to become champion for Ferrari at his fifth attempt. Think of Suzuka, and you think of Hakkinen, who'd won here in both 1998 and 1999 to wrap up the title. This time around, a Suzuka win wouldn't give him his third title in a row, but it would enable him to go to the final round in Malaysia with something to fight for.

Qualifying proved riveting as pole position passed backwards and forwards between Schumacher and Hakkinen until it came down in the German's favour, by just 0.009 seconds.

It was Hakkinen, though, who led into the first corner, avoiding a swerve from Schumacher. Hakkinen edged clear, while those behind fell away, with David Coulthard occupying third as Rubens Barrichello paid for a slow start that dropped him from fourth place to sixth, stuck behind the Williams of Ralf Schumacher and Jaguar's Eddie Irvine.

Rain had been forecast, but there was no sign of it when Hakkinen made the first of his two stops. With Schumacher unable to take the lead on the track, Ferrari put in more fuel during Schumacher's stop than McLaren had for Hakkinen. This meant that he was able to run a couple of extra laps. And it was to prove crucial.

With Schumacher having closed the gap from 2.5 seconds to 1 second, and a pair of Jaguars to be lapped as he approached his second stop, Hakkinen ducked into the pits. Almost immediately, drizzle turned into a shower as he rejoined on regular grooved tyres. This was a massive slice of misfortune, as Schumacher's extra laps before having to come in for his second pit stop would enable Ferrari to have rain tyres ready, and continued rain would mean that Hakkinen would have to pit again for rain tyres. However, the rain eased, Hakkinen lost time on rejoining in traffic and what Ferrari had reckoned would be a tight-run thing turned into a dream as Schumacher emerged from his second stop with a 5-second lead. All he had to do was finish the race without error, which he duly did, triggering rejoicing throughout Italy.

Hakkinen was gracious in defeat, with Coulthard a lonely third, easily clear of a recovering Barrichello who was 6.5 seconds clear of Jenson Button, who was the only other driver on the lead lap. Jacques Villeneuve fought his way past the Jaguars to give BAR a valuable point.

EARLY ADVANTAGE: Mika Hakkinen kept Michael Schumacher behind him early in the race ...

MALAYSIAN GP

MICHAEL MAKES IT NINE

RACE RESULTS

ROUND 17
AT SEPANG, OCTOBER 22, 2000
56 LAPS – 192.89 MILES

	Driver	Team
1	Michael Schumacher	Ferrari
2	David Coulthard	McLaren
3	Rubens Barrichello	Ferrari
4	Mika Hakkinen	McLaren
5	Jacques Villeneuve	BAR
6	Eddie Irvine	Jaguar

POLE . . . . M. Schumacher
1m 37.397s (127.31mph/204.88kph)

FASTEST LAP . . . . Hakkinen
1m 38.543s (125.83mph/202.50kph)

WEATHER . . . Sunny, dry & very hot

Michael Schumacher rounded out his outstanding title-winning campaign with his ninth win of the year for Ferrari, but he was pushed all the way to the finish line by McLaren's David Coulthard.

With Michael Schumacher having already secured the title at the previous round at Suzuka, Ferrari's aim was to complete its dream season by wrapping up the Constructors' Cup. The Italian team arrived at Sepang needing just three points to be sure of being the top team for the second year in succession, and Schumacher gave them the first advantage by claiming pole ahead of Mika Hakkinen, with Coulthard third and Rubens Barrichello fourth. Hakkinen was in front before they reached the first corner but, as at Indianapolis, McLaren was to suffer from a jump start, with the Finn having moved from his grid slot. He hit the brakes and was stationary when the starting lights went out, but the damage was done, and he would be called in for a stop-go penalty, dropping him to 18th and out of the reckoning. McLaren could now only pray for miracles. Still, at least Hakkinen made it around the first corner, which is more than could be said of Pedro Diniz, Nick Heidfeld and Pedro de la Rosa at the second corner.

Coulthard took over in the lead, but it soon became clear that he was running light and going for a two-stop strategy, while Schumacher was likely to stop only once. Anxious to pull away by the 0.5 seconds per lap that he needed, David ran wide at Turn 6 after a handful of laps. Although he regained the circuit, he'd picked up debris that would cause his engine temperature to rise. This forced an early pit stop, and let Schumacher into the lead. Thinking on their feet, Ferrari changed Schumacher to a two-stop strategy that was to keep him there, even though Coulthard closed fast in the final laps to finish just 0.7 seconds behind, after an uncomfortable ride caused by heat from his metal skidplates rising through the floor of the cockpit to roast his buttocks.

Barrichello was also in discomfort, struggling in the heat and humidity with flu, but he held on to third, still ahead of a flying Hakkinen. Fifth place went to Jacques Villeneuve to put BAR equal on points with Benetton, but behind on the countback rule, while Eddie Irvine claimed the final point to give Jaguar a little something to take with them into the close season. The bad luck in the Jaguar camp, as ever, hit Johnny Herbert, whose last race before quitting Formula One resulted in a high-speed crash into the barriers at Turn 4 when his rear suspension collapsed.

IN THE RED: Michael Schumacher joined in Ferrari's party spirit by donning a "stylish" red wig for the podium ceremony, with church bells across Italy being rung in celebration

NOTE

Drivers are listed according to their finishing position in each race.

** denotes that McLaren was not allowed to count the 10 points Hakkinen scored for winning the Austrian GP because of a technical discrepancy.

2000 FINAL TABLES
120

SCORING SYSTEM
First, **10 points**; second, **6 points**; third, **4 points**; fourth, **3 points**; fifth, **2 points**; sixth, **1 point**.

DRIVER	NAT.	CAR-ENGINE	1 March 12, Melbourne	2 March 26, Interlagos	3 April 9, Imola	4 April 23, Silverstone	5 May 7, Barcelona
Michael Schumacher	GER	Ferrari F1-2000	1	1F	1	3	5
Mika Hakkinen	FIN	McLaren-Mercedes MP4-15	RP	RP	2PF	2F	1
David Coulthard	GBR	McLaren-Mercedes MP4-15	R	D2	3	1	2
Rubens Barrichello	BRA	Ferrari F1-2000	2F	R	4	RP	3
Ralf Schumacher	GER	Williams-BMW FW22	3	5	R	4	
Giancarlo Fisichella	ITA	Benetton-Playlife B200	5	2	11	7	9
Jacques Villeneuve	CAN	BAR-Honda 02	4	R	5	16*	N
Jenson Button	GBR	Williams-BMW FW22	R	6	R	5	17
Heinz-Harald Frentzen	GER	Jordan-Mugen Honda EJ10	R	3	R	17*	6
Jarno Trulli	ITA	Jordan-Mugen Honda EJ10	R	4	15*	6	1
Mika Salo	FIN	Sauber-Petronas C19	D6	NS	6	8	
Jos Verstappen	HOL	Arrows-Supertec A21	R	7	14	R	N
Eddie Irvine	GBR	Jaguar R1	R	R	7	13	1
Ricardo Zonta	BRA	BAR-Honda 02	6	9	12	R	8
Alexander Wurz	AUT	Benetton-Playlife B200	7	R	9	9	
Pedro de la Rosa	SPA	Arrows-Supertec A21	R	8	R	R	
Jean Alesi	FRA	Prost-Peugeot AP03	R	R	R	10	
Luciano Burti	BRA	Jaguar R1					
Pedro Diniz	BRA	Sauber-Petronas C19	R	NS	8	11	N
Marc Gene	SPA	Minardi-Fondmetal M02	8	R	R	14	
Nick Heidfeld	GER	Prost-Peugeot AP03	9	R	R	R	1
Johnny Herbert	GBR	Jaguar R1	R	R	10	12	1
Gaston Mazzacane	ARG	Minardi-Fondmetal M02	R	10	13	15	

CONSTRUCTOR

		1 March 12, Melbourne	2 March 26, Interlagos	3 April 9, Imola	4 April 23, Silverstone	5 May 7, Barcelona
1	Ferrari	16	10	13	4	
2	McLaren-Mercedes	-	-	10	16	
3	Williams-BMW	4	3	-	5	
4	Benetton-Playlife	2	6	-	-	
5	BAR-Honda	4	-	2	-	
6	Jordan-Mugen Honda	-	7	-	1	
7	Arrows-Supertec	-	-	-	-	
8	Sauber-Petronas	-	-	1	-	
9	Jaguar	-	-	-	-	
	Minardi-Fondmetal	-	-	-	-	
	Prost-Peugeot	-	-	-	-	

SYMBOLS

D	denotes disqualified
F	denotes fastest lap
NC	denotes not classified (i.e. still running at the end of the race, but without having covered sufficient distance)
NP	denotes did not practise
NQ	denotes did not qualify
NS	denotes did not start the race
P	denotes pole position
R	denotes retired from race
*	denotes classified but not running at finish
-	denotes did not score (in the Constructors' Cup)

7 June 4, Monaco	8 June 18, Montreal	9 July 2, Magny-Cours	10 July 16, A1-Ring	11 July 30, Hockenheim	12 August 13, Hungaroring	13 August 27, Spa-Francorchamps	14 September 10, Monza	15 September 24, Indianapolis	16 October 8, Suzuka	17 October 22, Sepang	Points total
RP	1P	RP	R	R	2P	2	1P	1P	1P	1P	108
6F	4F	2	1P	2	1F	1P	2F	R	2F	4F	89
1	7	1F	2F	3P	3	4	R	5F	3	2	73
2	2	3	3	1F	4	RF	R	2	4	3	62
R	14*	5	R	7	5	3	3	R	R	R	24
3	3	9	R	R	R	R	11	R	14	9	18
7	15*	4	4	8	12	7	R	4	6	5	17
R	11	8	5	4	9	5	R	R	5	R	12
10*	R	7	R	R	6	6	R	3	R	R	11
R	6	6	R	9	7	R	R	R	13	12	6
5	R	10	6	5	10	9	7	R	10	8	6
R	5	R	R	R	13	15	4	R	R	10	5
4	13	13	NP	10	8	10	R	7	8	6	4
R	8	R	R	R	14	12	6	6	9	R	3
R	9	R	10	R	11	13	5	10	R	7	2
NS	R	R	R	6	10	16	R	R	12	R	2
R	R	14	R	R	R	R	12	R	R	11	
			11								
R	10	11	9	R	R	11	8	8	11	R	
R	16*	15	8	R	15	14	9	12	R	R	
8	R	12	R	12	R	R	R	9	R	R	
9	R	R	7	R	R	8	R	11	7	R	
R	12	R	12	11	R	17	10	R	15	13	

7 June 4, Monaco	8 June 18, Montreal	9 July 2, Magny-Cours	10 July 16, A1-Ring	11 July 30, Hockenheim	12 August 13, Hungaroring	13 August 27, Spa-Francorchamps	14 September 10, Monza	15 September 24, Indianapolis	16 October 8, Suzuka	17 October 22, Sepang	Points total
6	16	4	4	10	9	6	10	16	13	14	170
11	3	16	6**	10	14	13	6	2	10	9	152
-	-	2	2	3	2	6	4	-	2	-	36
4	4	-	-	-	-	-	2	-	-	2	20
-	-	3	3	-	-	-	1	4	1	2	20
-	1	1	-	-	1	1	-	4	-	-	17
-	2	-	-	1	-	-	3	-	-	-	7
2	-	-	1	2	-	-	-	-	-	-	6
3	-	-	-	-	-	-	-	-	-	1	4

MOST GRAND PRIX STARTS

DRIVERS

256	Riccardo Patrese	ITA	145	Mika Hakkinen	FIN
210	Gerhard Berger	AUT		Michael Schumacher	GER
208	Andrea de Cesaris	ITA	144	Emerson Fittipaldi	BRA
204	Nelson Piquet	BRA	135	Jean-Pierre Jarier	FRA
199	Alain Prost	FRA	132	Eddie Cheever	USA
194	Michele Alboreto	ITA		Clay Regazzoni	SUI
187	Nigel Mansell	GBR	130	Rubens Barrichello	BRA
184	Jean Alesi	FRA	128	Mario Andretti	USA
176	Graham Hill	GBR	126	Jack Brabham	AUS
175	Jacques Laffite	FRA	123	Ronnie Peterson	SWE
171	Niki Lauda	AUT	119	Pierluigi Martini	ITA
163	Thierry Boutsen	BEL	116	Jacky Ickx	BEL
162	Johnny Herbert	GBR		Damon Hill	GBR
161	Ayrton Senna	BRA		Alan Jones	AUS
158	Martin Brundle	GBR	114	Heinz-Harald Frentzen	GER
152	John Watson	GBR		Keke Rosberg	FIN
149	Rene Arnoux	FRA		Patrick Tambay	FRA
147	Derek Warwick	GBR	113	Eddie Irvine	GBR
146	Carlos Reutemann	ARG	112	Denny Hulme	NZL
				Jody Scheckter	RSA

CONSTRUCTORS

636	Ferrari	394	Brabham	230	March
509	McLaren	392	Prost	197	BRM
490	Lotus	354	Arrows	163	Jordan
428	Williams	300	Benetton	132	Osella
418	Tyrrell	254	Minardi	129	Cooper

MOST WINS

DRIVERS

51	Alain Prost	FRA		Alan Jones	AUS
44	Michael Schumacher	GER		Carlos Reutemann	ARG
41	Ayrton Senna	BRA	11	Jacques Villeneuve	CDN
31	Nigel Mansell	GBR	10	Gerhard Berger	AUT
27	Jackie Stewart	GBR		James Hunt	GBR
25	Jim Clark	GBR		Ronnie Peterson	SWE
	Niki Lauda	AUT		Jody Scheckter	RSA
24	Juan Manuel Fangio	ARG	9	David Coulthard	GBR
23	Nelson Piquet	BRA	8	Denny Hulme	NZL
22	Damon Hill	GBR		Jacky Ickx	BEL
18	Mika Hakkinen	FIN	7	Rene Arnoux	FRA
16	Stirling Moss	GBR	6	Tony Brooks	GBR
14	Jack Brabham	AUS		Jacques Laffite	FRA
	Emerson Fittipaldi	BRA		Riccardo Patrese	FRA
	Graham Hill	GBR		Jochen Rindt	AUT
13	Alberto Ascari	ITA		John Surtees	GBR
12	Mario Andretti	USA		Gilles Villeneuve	CDN

CONSTRUCTORS

135	Ferrari	15	Renault		Wolf
130	McLaren	10	Alfa Romeo	2	Honda
102	Williams	9	Ligier	1	Eagle
79	Lotus		Maserati		Hesketh
35	Brabham		Matra		Penske
27	Benetton		Mercedes		Porsche
23	Tyrrell		Vanwall		Shadow
17	BRM	3	Jordan		Stewart
16	Cooper		March		

AN EXPERIENCED TRIO: Mansell, Senna and Patrese at Adelaide in 1992

MOST WINS IN ONE SEASON

DRIVERS

9	Nigel Mansell	GBR	1992		Ayrton Senna	BRA	1991
	M Schumacher	GER	1995		J Villeneuve	CDN	1997
	M Schumacher	GER	2000	6	Mario Andretti	USA	1978
8	Mika Hakkinen	FIN	1998		Alberto Ascari	ITA	1952
	Damon Hill	GBR	1996		Jim Clark	GBR	1965
	M Schumacher	GER	1994		Juan M Fangio	ARG	1954
	Ayrton Senna	BRA	1988		Damon Hill	GBR	1994
7	Jim Clark	GBR	1963		James Hunt	GBR	1976
	Alain Prost	FRA	1984		Nigel Mansell	GBR	1987
	Alain Prost	FRA	1988		M Schumacher	GER	1998
	Alain Prost	FRA	1993		Ayrton Senna	BRA	1989
					Ayrton Senna	BRA	1990

CONSTRUCTORS

15	McLaren	1988		Williams	1997	Ferrari	1976
12	McLaren	1984	7	Ferrari	1952	Ferrari	1979
	Williams	1996		Ferrari	1953	Ferrari	1990
11	Benetton	1995		Lotus	1963	Ferrari	1996
10	Ferrari	2000		Lotus	1973	Ferrari	1998
	McLaren	1989		McLaren	1999	Ferrari	1999
	Williams	1992		McLaren	2000	Lotus	1965
	Williams	1993		Tyrrell	1971	Lotus	1970
9	McLaren	1998		Williams	1991	Matra	1969
	Williams	1986		Williams	1994	McLaren	1976
	Williams	1987	6	Alfa Romeo	1950	McLaren	1985
8	Benetton	1994		Alfa Romeo	1951	McLaren	1990
	Lotus	1978		Cooper	1960	Vanwall	1958
	McLaren	1991		Ferrari	1975	Williams	1980

MOST CONSECUTIVE WINS

9	Alberto Ascari	ITA 1952/53			Damon Hill	GBR 1995/96	
5	Jack Brabham	AUS	1960		Alain Prost	FRA	1993
	Jim Clark	GBR	1965		Jochen Rindt	AUT	1970
	Nigel Mansell	GBR	1992		M Schumacher	GER	1994
4	Jack Brabham	AUS	1966		M Schumacher	GER	2000
	Jim Clark	GBR	1963		Ayrton Senna	BRA	1988
	Juan M Fangio	ARG 1953/54			Ayrton Senna	BRA	1991

EARLY-DAY HEROES: Luigi Villoresi and World Champion Alberto Ascari share the garlands in Switzerland in 1953

GRAND PRIX STARTS WITHOUT A WIN

208	Andrea de Cesaris	ITA	109	Philippe Alliot	FRA
158	Martin Brundle	GBR	99	Pedro Diniz	BRA
147	Derek Warwick	GBR	97	Chris Amon	NZL
135	Jean-Pierre Jarier	FRA	95	Ukyo Katayama	JAP
132	Eddie Cheever	USA	94	Mika Salo	FIN
119	Pierluigi Martini	ITA	93	Ivan Capelli	ITA

MOST FASTEST LAPS

DRIVERS

41	Alain Prost	FRA		Ayrton Senna	BRA
40	Michael Schumacher	GER	15	Clay Regazzoni	SUI
30	Nigel Mansell	GBR		Jackie Stewart	GBR
28	Jim Clark	GBR	14	David Coulthard	GBR
25	Niki Lauda	AUT		Jacky Ickx	BEL
23	Juan Manuel Fangio	ARG	13	Alberto Ascari	ITA
	Nelson Piquet	BRA		Alan Jones	AUS
22	Mika Hakkinen	FIN		Riccardo Patrese	ITA
21	Gerhard Berger	AUT	12	Rene Arnoux	FRA
20	Stirling Moss	GBR		Jack Brabham	AUS
19	Damon Hill	GBR	11	John Surtees	GBR

CONSTRUCTORS

143	Ferrari	20	Tyrrell	12	Matra		
111	Williams	18	Renault	11	Prost		
101	McLaren	15	BRM	9	Mercedes		
71	Lotus		Maserati	7	March		
40	Brabham	14	Alfa Romeo	6	Vanwall		
35	Benetton	13	Cooper				

MOST POLE POSITIONS

DRIVERS

65	Ayrton Senna	BRA	16	Stirling Moss	GBR
33	Jim Clark	GBR	14	Alberto Ascari	ITA
	Alain Prost	FRA		James Hunt	GBR
32	Nigel Mansell	GBR		Ronnie Peterson	SWE
	Michael Schumacher	GER	13	Jack Brabham	AUS
29	Juan Manuel Fangio	ARG		Graham Hill	GBR
26	Mika Hakkinen	FIN		Jacky Ickx	BEL
24	Niki Lauda	AUT		Jacques Villeneuve	CDN
	Nelson Piquet	BRA	12	Gerhard Berger	AUT
20	Damon Hill	GBR	10	David Coulthard	GBR
18	Mario Andretti	USA		Jochen Rindt	AUT
	Rene Arnoux	FRA	8	Riccardo Patrese	ITA
17	Jackie Stewart	GBR		John Surtees	GBR

CONSTRUCTORS

137	Ferrari	14	Tyrrell	7	Vanwall		
110	McLaren	12	Alfa Romeo	5	March		
108	Williams	11	BRM	4	Matra		
107	Lotus		Cooper	3	Shadow		
39	Brabham	10	Maserati	2	Jordan		
31	Renault	9	Prost		Lancia		
16	Benetton	8	Mercedes	1	Stewart		

IN ONE SEASON, DRIVERS

14	Nigel Mansell	GBR	1992			Nelson Piquet	BRA	1984
13	Alain Prost	FRA	1993			M Schumacher	GER	2000
	Ayrton Senna	BRA	1988		8	Mario Andretti	USA	1978
	Ayrton Senna	BRA	1989			James Hunt	GBR	1976
11	Mika Hakkinen	FIN	1999			Nigel Mansell	GBR	1987
10	Ayrton Senna	BRA	1990			Ayrton Senna	BRA	1986
	J Villeneuve	CDN	1997			Ayrton Senna	BRA	1991
9	Mika Hakkinen	FIN	1998		7	Mario Andretti	USA	1977
	Damon Hill	GBR	1996			Jim Clark	GBR	1963
	Niki Lauda	AUT	1974			Damon Hill	GBR	1995
	Niki Lauda	AUT	1975			Ayrton Senna	BRA	1985
	Ronnie Peterson	SWE	1973					

IN ONE SEASON, CONSTRUCTORS

15	McLaren	1988		Williams	1987	Lotus	1973
	McLaren	1989		Williams	1995	McLaren	1991
	Williams	1992		Williams	1996	Renault	1982
	Williams	1993	11	McLaren	1999	9 Brabham	1984
12	Lotus	1978		Williams	1997	Ferrari	1975
	McLaren	1990	10	Ferrari	1974		
	McLaren	1998		Ferrari	2000		

THE FIRST OF MANY: Michael Schumacher celebrates the first of his 44 Grand Prix wins at Spa in 1992

MOST POINTS

(this figure is gross tally, ie. including scores that were later dropped)

DRIVERS

798.5	Alain Prost	FRA	294	David Coulthard	GBR	
678	Michael Schumacher	GER	289	Graham Hill	GBR	
614	Ayrton Senna	BRA	281	Emerson Fittipaldi	BRA	
485.5	Nelson Piquet	BRA		Riccardo Patrese	ITA	
482	Nigel Mansell	GBR	277.5	Juan Manuel Fangio	ARG	
420.5	Niki Lauda	AUT	274	Jim Clark	GBR	
385	Gerhard Berger	AUT	261	Jack Brabham	AUS	
383	Mika Hakkinen	FIN	255	Jody Scheckter	RSA	
360	Damon Hill	GBR	248	Denny Hulme	NZL	
	Jackie Stewart	GBR	236	Jean Alesi	FRA	
310	Carlos Reutemann	ARG	228	Jacques Laffite	FRA	

CONSTRUCTORS

2524.5	Ferrari	439	BRM	155	Matra
2480.5	McLaren	420	Prost	90	Sauber
2031.5	Williams	333	Cooper	79	Wolf
1352	Lotus	312	Renault	67.5	Shadow
867.5	Benetton	233	Jordan	57	Vanwall
854	Brabham	171.5	March	54	Surtees
617	Tyrrell	164	Arrows	51	Stewart

PACE AND GRACE: Juan Manuel Fangio looks unflustered as he races to his greatest ever win - the 1957 German GP

MOST DRIVER TITLES

5	Juan Manuel Fangio	ARG		Giuseppe Farina	ITA
4	Alain Prost	FRA		Mike Hawthorn	GBR
3	Jack Brabham	AUS		Damon Hill	GBR
	Niki Lauda	AUT		Phil Hill	USA
	Nelson Piquet	BRA		Denis Hulme	NZL
	Michael Schumacher	GER		James Hunt	GBR
	Ayrton Senna	BRA		Alan Jones	AUS
	Jackie Stewart	GBR		Nigel Mansell	GBR
2	Alberto Ascari	ITA		Jochen Rindt	AUT
	Jim Clark	GBR		Keke Rosberg	FIN
	Emerson Fittipaldi	BRA		Jody Scheckter	RSA
	Mika Hakkinen	FIN		John Surtees	GBR
	Graham Hill	GBR		Jacques Villeneuve	CDN
1	Mario Andretti	USA			

MOST CONSTRUCTORS' TITLES

10	Ferrari	2	Brabham		Matra
9	Williams		Cooper		Tyrrell
8	McLaren	1	Benetton		Vanwall
7	Lotus		BRM		

				March 4, AUSTRALIAN GP	March 18, MALAYSIAN GP	April 1, BRAZILIAN GP	April 15, SAN MARINO GP	April 29, SPANISH GP	May 13, AUSTRIAN GP
1	Ferrari	MICHAEL SCHUMACHER	GER						
2	Ferrari	RUBENS BARRICHELLO	BRA						
3	McLaren	MIKA HAKKINEN	FIN						
4	McLaren	DAVID COULTHARD	GBR						
5	Williams	RALF SCHUMACHER	GER						
6	Williams	JUAN PABLO MONTOYA	COL						
7	Benetton	GIANCARLO FISICHELLA	ITA						
8	Benetton	JENSON BUTTON	GBR						
9	BAR	JACQUES VILLENEUVE	CDN						
10	BAR	OLIVIER PANIS	FRA						
11	Jordan	HEINZ-HARALD FRENTZEN	GER						
12	Jordan	JARNO TRULLI	ITA						
14	Arrows	JOS VERSTAPPEN	HOL						
15	Arrows	PEDRO DE LA ROSA	SPA						
16	Sauber	NICK HEIDFELD	GER						
17	Sauber	KIMI RAIKKONEN	FIN						
18	Jaguar	EDDIE IRVINE	GBR						
19	Jaguar	LUCIANO BURTI	BRA						
20	Minardi	tbc							
21	Minardi	tbc							
22	Prost	JEAN ALESI	FRA						
23	Prost	tbc							

WORLD CHAMPIONSHIP F1

FIA FORMULA ONE
WORLD
CHAMPIONSHIP
127

May 27, MONACO GP	June 10, CANADIAN GP	June 24, EUROPEAN GP	July 1, FRENCH GP	July 15, BRITISH GP	July 29, GERMAN GP	August 19, HUNGARIAN GP	September 2, BELGIAN GP	September 16, ITALIAN GP	September 30, UNITED STATES GP	October 14, JAPANESE GP

AND FINALLY...

The news that Murray Walker will be retiring at the end of this World Championship season comes as a massive blow to Britain's millions of Formula One fans. However, after 52 years behind the microphone at the end of the 2001 season, and with 77 years on the clock, Murray has decided that the time has come to take life a little more easily. So, race fans, make the most of this final World Championship accompanied by Murray's hugely excited delivery that is synonymous with Formula One, with Murray guiding you through every incident as though his life depended on it. Indeed, Murray cares so much for the sport that he probably thinks that his life *does* depend on it, from whenever a Grand Prix goes under starter's orders until the chequered flag is brought down on the winner almost two hours later.

Murray and motorsport are so intertwined that it is hard to imagine one without the other. Son of a motorcycle racing champion, Murray followed his father Graham into commentary, moving swiftly from hillclimbs to commentate on the British Grand Prix for the first time in 1949. A full generation of motorsport fans grew up listening to his commentaries on everything from racing to rallycross before Formula One became a regular on our television screens in the late 1970s. And it was at this point that Murray single-handedly transformed Formula One from something for the die-hard fans to something for every sport fan, with his ever-enthusiastic delivery making more and more people want to watch. Formula One with Murray is not a sport of cars going round and round in circles, but one in which the contestants are real people doing gladiatorial deeds, with the human side so important in giving Formula One a face.

Alone at the helm for so long, Murray wasn't too sure that he wanted a second-in-command alongside him in the commentary box when 1976 World Champion James Hunt was introduced once he'd retired from the cockpit. However, having someone who had been there and done it, someone off whom Murray could bounce ideas, worked wonderfully, and a famous double act was formed. Martin Brundle followed in Hunt's footsteps when ITV took over and displayed all the skills of a seasoned professional from the very outset, making the Murray and Martin pairing one of the best in all sports. Knowledgeable, informative and ever-entertaining, they never miss a thing between them, which is one of the reasons why the popularity of Formula One continues to grow with every passing year.

Drivers will come and drivers will go, but Murray will forever be remembered as the voice of Formula One. No man in the history of the sport has done as much to make it so popular. He will be greatly missed and all of us who were brought up on his commentaries wish Murray a happy and well-earned retirement.